Nonfiction
Grade 5

Introduction

Instilling in reluctant readers the desire to read can be one of the most difficult tasks for an educator. Success—having your once reluctant reader *ask* for books—can be one of the most rewarding experiences a teacher can have.

The stories in this book have been written with one purpose. They are all written to capture and hold the interest of all readers—whether they think they like to read or not. These stories are also nonfiction. Good readers who may not normally choose nonfiction to read will find these stories irresistible. They will learn that nonfiction stories can be as exciting, mysterious, thrilling, and moving as any piece of fiction. These stories tell of courage, hard work, strength, commitment, faith, hope, luck, sorrow, happiness, and mystery. They begin with a hook that draws the reader in. Then they tell their story quickly so the reader does not lose interest. Before they know it, students have read *with interest* and *learned* from nonfiction!

Organization

The stories in this book fall into eight categories: Challenges, Rescues, Firsts, Adventures, Mysteries, Escapes, Disasters, and Heroes. Each category has between two and six stories.

Each story is followed by four short activities to test students' comprehension. The activities are titled *Do You Remember?, Exploring Words, Critical Thinking,* and *Express Yourself. Do You Remember?* asks literal questions and requires the student to distinguish between true and false statements. Students will also find multiple choice questions in this section. *Exploring Words* helps students with vocabulary through cloze, completing sentences, finding like meanings, and crossword puzzles. The *Critical Thinking* exercises include cause and effect, fact and opinion, main ideas, sequence, and drawing conclusions. *Express Yourself* includes letter writing, writing news articles, journal entries, and creative writing. Students will draw conclusions and use their abilities for extending and evaluating meaning as they write.

There is a Progress Chart on Page 6. If this is distributed to the students, they can keep track of how they are doing on the exercises. You will note that for the *Express Yourself* exercises, it is suggested that the teacher give a score of 1 to 5, 5 being the best score for the writing.

Use

Nonfiction is designed for independent use by students. Copies of the stories and activities can be given to individuals, pairs of students, or small groups for completion. They can also be used as a center activity.

To begin, determine the implementation that fits your students' needs and your classroom structure. The following plan suggests a format for this implementation.

1. **Explain** the purpose of the activities to your class.

2. **Review** the mechanics of how you want students to work with the stories and exercises. Do you want to introduce the subject of each article? Do you want to tap into the students' prior knowledge of the subject and create a word web?

3. **Do** a practice activity together. Review with students how to use context to figure out the meaning of a word. Remind them to use a dictionary when the context is not enough to figure out the meaning.

4. **Determine** how you will monitor the Assessments. Each assessment can be given individually, or all four pages can be given as a pre-test and a post-test. If given individually, you may give one page before the students begin to work with the book, one or two at the halfway point, and one or two after completion of the book. Tests can be administered individually, to a group that has successfully completed the activities, or to the whole class. The tests are not meant to determine students' knowledge of the content of all the stories, but to determine students' abilities to draw information from nonfiction writing.

5. **Assure** students that this work is for practice purposes. Through this work they will become better readers in all subjects. Go over the Letter to Students with them and answer any questions that arise.

Additional Notes

1. **Parent Communication** Use the Letter to Parents, and encourage students to share the Letter to Students with their parents. Decide if you want to keep the activity pages and Assessments in portfolios for conferencing, or if you want students to take them home as they are completed.

2. **Bulletin Boards** Display selected research projects and writing assignments in your classroom.

3. **Have Fun** Encourage students to discuss the stories and their reactions to them. Encourage any constructive debate or discussions of personal experiences that may arise from the reading.

Dear Parents:

Our class will be working with a book of nonfiction reading. The book has 28 stories of real-life challenges, rescues, firsts, adventures, mysteries, escapes, disasters, and heroes. They were written to interest every reader. Even students who do not read often will enjoy these exciting stories. If students are interested, they will get more out of their reading. It also helps students to talk about their reading. Ask your child about what he or she is reading and share your own knowledge about the events.

Each story is followed by exercises to test students' understanding of their reading. These exercises and the reading may be done in class or at home. If your child brings work home, please consider the following suggestions:

- **Provide a quiet place to work.**
- **If your child is reading, help your child find the meanings of difficult words through the context of the story. Discuss the story.**
- **Go over the directions for the exercises together.**
- **Check the lesson when it is complete. Note areas of improvement as well as concern.**

Thank you for being involved in your child's learning. Your efforts will encourage your child and promote a lifelong love of learning.

Cordially,

Dear Student:

Our class is going to be working with a book of exciting real-life stories. These stories are all real, and they are all amazing. There are mysteries, heroes, challenges, and rescues. There are adventures, escapes, disasters, and firsts.

Find out what happened when explorers went to the South Pole for the first time. Read about rescues at sea, and a young girl who saved her family from a fire. Learn about the first woman doctor in the U.S. Army, and mysterious giant drawings in the desert. Learn about a daring balloon escape to freedom and an earthquake in San Francisco.

After each story, there are some short exercises. These will tell you how well you read. Chances are you will remember these interesting stories. Read carefully, and you will do well. You may take them home as homework. Remember to work in a quiet place. Work away from the television and radio. You will be able to concentrate on your work.

Happy Reading!

Cordially,

Name_____   Date_____

Nonfiction Grade 5
Progress Chart

Story Titles	Do You Remember?	Exploring Words	Critical Thinking	Express Yourself	Your Score
Bottom of the World				X	__/17
Life in the Wild				X	__/20
Skiing Down Everest			X		__/19
A Ship in Flames			X		__/20
Do or Die!				X	__/17
Abandon Ship!				X	__/14
Trapped in a Well				X	__/18
Doctor Under Fire				X	__/18
Reaching for the Sky			X		__/17
Running for the Gold				X	__/18
Race Across Alaska			X		__/20
Marco Polo				X	__/16
Flight of the Eagle				X	__/20
The Kon-Tiki			X		__/18
The Secrets of Stonehenge				X	__/16
Designs in the Desert			X		__/23
An Island of Giants				X	__/16
Triangle of Fear				X	__/15
What Happened to Amelia?			X		__/19
A Spaceship Adventure				X	__/16
Balloon Ride to Freedom			X		__/15
Lawyer Turns Outlaw				X	__/12
Washed Away!				X	__/23
A City in Ruins			X		__/21
Nightmare at Sea				X	__/14
Hurricane Warning!			X		__/18
Doctor for the Poor			X		__/16
Beating the Odds			X		__/21

To Find Your Score:

1. Count the number of correct answers you have for each activity.

2. Write these numbers in the boxes in the chart.

3. Ask your teacher to give you a score (maximum of 5) for **Express Yourself.**

4. Add up the numbers to get a final score.

Assessment 1
Nonfiction Grade 5

Directions: Read the selection. Then complete the exercise below.

Fourteen-year-old Karen Hartsock woke one night to find her house on fire. Her parents' room was downstairs, but her brother and sisters were upstairs with her. She was worried about them.

Her younger sister Norma was eleven. When Karen yelled to her, she came out of her room, but she didn't know what to do. Karen ran with her to the burning stairway; it was the only way down. She pulled her sister through the flames and went back for her brother. She found Johnny sleeping in his bed. She wrapped him in a blanket and hurried down the stairs with him.

Karen's hair and skin were being badly burned, but she did not stop. Her father wanted her out of the house, but she thought she needed to help her twelve-year-old sister, Loretta. As she headed up the stairs, they collapsed. Mr. Hartsock was recovering from a heart operation, but with all his strength, he pulled Karen from the pile of burning wood and pulled her from the house. Karen didn't know it, but Loretta was already outside.

Karen suffered severe burns all over her body and took many months to recover, but she never regretted saving her family from the flames.

Directions: Choose the best ending for each sentence. Write the letter in the blank.

_____ **1.** Karen Hartsock was

   a. fourteen years old.   b. twelve years old.   c. nine years old.

_____ **2.** Karen saved her brother and sister from

   a. drowning.   b. burning.   c. falling.

_____ **3.** Karen started back up the stairs the third time for

   a. Loretta.   b. Johnny.   c. her father.

_____ **4.** Because of the burns on her body, Karen Hartsock

   a. fainted.   b. died.   c. took many months to recover.

_____ **5.** Karen was badly burned, but she never felt

   a. sad.   b. regret.   c. ugly.

Assessment 2
Nonfiction Grade 5

Directions: Read the selection. Then complete the exercise below.

Libby Riddles had a lifelong dream of being the first woman ever to win the Iditarod Trail Sled Dog Race. This 1,172-mile race went from Anchorage, Alaska, to Nome, Alaska. This was not the first time she had entered the race, but this time she was out to win.

In the first few days, Riddles made good time. She often drove 14 miles without resting. She did stop to feed her dogs often and to check their paws. Although the dogs wore nylon boots, their paws often were cut or frozen. Libby took good care of them. Libby did not rest often. At times, she became so tired that she fell asleep while driving the dogs. The dogs were well trained and would continue on the trail while she slept. Other drivers, or mushers, fell asleep, too. They all wanted the $50,000 prize money.

The mushers had faced several days of snowstorms. By the ninth day, they also faced -40 to -53 degree temperatures and high winds. Most mushers took long breaks to recover from the harsh conditions, but Riddles moved on. On the fifteenth day, a blizzard had forced all mushers to stop. Riddles decided to move on in the blizzard, but was also forced to stop after only three hours. For 11 hours she lay in her sleeping bag, and her dogs curled up into tight balls while the storm raged around them.

Finally, Riddles decided to try again. She worried that the other mushers would catch up to her. She decided to take a shortcut across Norton Sound. It was a risky decision. Out on the ice there were no trail markings and no shelter. If the ice broke, Riddles and her dogs might be killed. For hours she struggled across the bay, but she made it to the other side safely.

Finally, 17 days after she had started out, Libby Riddles crossed the finish line. All of her hard work had paid off. She had indeed become the first woman ever to win the Iditarod.

Directions: Pretend that you are Libby Riddles. You have just crossed the finish line of the Iditarod Trail Sled Dog Race. Write a letter to a friend telling him or her how you feel. Use the back of this paper or another sheet.

Assessment 3
Nonfiction Grade 5

Directions: Read the selection. Then complete the exercises below.

In the desert of Peru, a country in South America, there are 600-foot-long lizards and 900-foot-tall birds. They are not real animals, but are drawings in the sand. The Nazca Indians made these drawings about 2,000 years ago.

The lines were made by scraping away stones to show the yellow soil beneath. Most of the lines are only a few inches wide. Stones are piled along both sides of the lines. Some of the lines are more than five miles long, and one is almost 40 miles long! It is believed that all the work was done by hand.

The Nazca lines are hard to see standing on the ground. Most of the shapes can only be recognized from high above the ground. Why did the Nazca Indians make the drawings so large? And how did they see them from above the ground? No one really knows the answers to these questions. It is thought that the Nazcas actually had hot-air balloons. A very light, fine cloth that would have worked as a balloon has been found in Nazcan tombs. Also, large circles of blackened rocks at the ends of many of the lines suggest that they made fires to fill the balloons with hot air.

A. Directions: Underline the two most important ideas from the story.

1. The Nazca Indians made giant drawings in the desert.

2. They probably made hot-air balloons to see their drawings.

3. Scientists found a light, fine cloth in Nazcan tombs.

4. The reason the Nazcans made the drawings is not known.

5. One of the drawings is of a 900-foot-tall bird.

B. Directions: Write *fact* or *opinion* next to each sentence.

_____ 1. The Nazcans should have explained the reasons for their drawings.

_____ 2. No one really knows why the drawings are so large.

_____ 3. Scientists should not have looked in the Nazcans' tombs.

_____ 4. One of the lines is almost 40 miles long.

_____ 5. The Nazca Indians made the drawings about 2,000 years ago.

Name_____   Date_____

Assessment 4
Nonfiction Grade 5

Directions: Read the selection. Then complete the exercises below.

Gunter Wetzel and Peter Strelzyk wanted to escape from East Germany to West Germany. East Germany was a communist country and the people did not have much freedom there. They had to think of a way to escape. They decided to use a hot-air balloon to fly them and their families to freedom.

Though neither man knew anything about balloons, they were determined to succeed. They bought 880 yards of material, saying it was for tents for a summer camp, and began to sew it together. When it was done, they tried to fill it with air, but the air just leaked out. It was the wrong kind of cloth.

They went and bought more material.

This time they said they belonged to a sailing club. Then Wetzel changed his mind about escaping. It was too risky. Strelzyk sewed the second balloon himself. He and his family tried to use it, but it, too, failed. After they were in the air, fog made the material damp and heavy, and the balloon came back down before they had crossed the border. They had to leave the balloon stuck in the trees. The police found the balloon and vowed to put its owners in prison.

Now Strelzyk needed to hurry. He asked Wetzel to help him one more time. This time, in one of the largest hot-air balloons ever made in Europe, both families escaped to West Germany.

A. Directions: Write the best ending for each sentence.

1. Wetzel and Strelzyk wanted to escape East Germany because_____

_____.

2. The first balloon failed because _____

_____.

3. Wetzel changed his mind because_____

_____.

B. Directions: Write *true* or *false* in front of each sentence.

_____ **1.** Wetzel and Strelzyk were Communists.

_____ **2.** They bought 880 yards of fabric for the first balloon.

_____ **3.** The second balloon did not make it to West Germany.

_____ **4.** Strelzyk was arrested by the police when they found the balloon.

_____ **5.** Both families made it to freedom in West Germany.

Bottom of the World

Roald Amundsen, a Norwegian explorer, smiled happily to himself. He had planned his trip to the North Pole carefully. He had mapped out the route and gathered plenty of supplies. But in September 1909, he heard that an explorer named Robert Peary had just reached the North Pole.

"There is no point in making the journey now," thought Amundsen. "Peary has beaten me to it." Then he had a new thought. "I'll go to the South Pole instead! No one has been there yet!"

Amundsen did not tell anyone about his change in plans. He knew that another explorer was already planning a trip to the South Pole. This explorer was an Englishman named Robert Scott. By keeping his plans a secret, he hoped to get a head start on Scott.

In the summer of 1910, Amundsen left Norway. Three of his crew knew where they were headed. The other five still thought they were going to the North Pole. When they reached Portugal, Amundsen told them the truth. The men all liked the idea of going to the South Pole. They hoped to be the first ones to get there. If they were, it would bring glory to themselves and to Norway. When the group reached Australia, Amundsen sent a message to Robert Scott. He told Scott that he was on his way to the South Pole.

Amundsen and his men continued on to Antarctica. In January 1911, they reached the Ross Ice Shelf. This is a huge field of ice on the edge of Antarctica, 788 miles from the South Pole.

"We will camp here for the winter," Amundsen told his men. "We can't go any farther until spring. Scott will have to wait for spring, too. No one can travel when it is this cold."

Indeed, it was incredibly cold. The temperature often hit 70 degrees below zero. The wind made it seem even colder. Six months later, in September, the temperature began to rise. On September 7, it seemed almost warm. Amundsen announced that they would leave the next day.

"I don't think we should," said Frederick Johansen. "I don't think winter is over yet. In September, Antarctic temperatures often rise for a few days. But spring does not really come until October."

"Nonsense," snapped Amundsen. "We will leave tomorrow."

The men did as Amundsen ordered. On September 8, they set off on dog sleds. Amundsen was thinking about Scott every step of the way. After three days, the temperature suddenly dropped. It was -56 degrees. The men and dogs struggled against the cold. Their breath froze as it left their mouths, and the dogs' paws began to bleed. The next day was even colder. It was -67 degrees. The men and the dogs did not have much strength in such weather. Johansen had been right; winter was not over.

On September 14, the men turned around and headed back to camp. When they got there, most of them were in bad shape. Their hands, feet, noses, and chins were frozen. Amundsen waited in camp until the weather got warmer. On October 20, he couldn't wait any longer—he had to get moving! The weather was pleasant. Amundsen ordered his men to pack up and head out.

This time the good weather lasted less than two days, then the temperature dropped to -30. But this time Amundsen did not turn back. This was his last chance. By November 20, the food supply was low. Amundsen picked out the 24 weakest dogs to use as food. That left 18 dogs to pull three sleds. Next, a blizzard struck. Day after day, the wind and snow blocked out everything. Each step was difficult; there were many hidden cracks in the ice. If the men stepped into one, they might fall to an icy death. Once one of Amundsen's men thought he saw Scott up ahead. It turned out to be his imagination. But the fear of losing the race made Amundsen move faster.

On December 8, they were 100 miles from the South Pole. No one had ever been closer. By December 13, they were only 15 miles away, and on December 14, 1911, they finally reached their goal. Amundsen and his men stood at the very bottom of the world. There were no footprints and there was no English flag. They had beaten Scott to the South Pole!

Amundsen and his men stuck the flag of Norway into the snow. They also left a short note for Scott. Then they turned around and headed home. Thirty-five days later, Robert Scott found the flag and note waiting for him. Robert Scott and his men died on the return journey. Amundsen and his men were luckier. They made it back, and they returned to Norway as heroes!

Do You Remember?

In the blank, write the letter of the best ending for each sentence.

_____ **1.** Roald Amundsen was from
   a. England.   b. Australia.   c. Norway.

_____ **2.** Amundsen and his men spent the winter
   a. at the North Pole.   b. on the Ross Ice Shelf.   c. in Portugal.

_____ **3.** Amundsen and his men killed 24
   a. birds.   b. seals.   c. dogs.

_____ **4.** At the South Pole, Amundsen left
   a. a flag.   b. a sled.   c. an igloo.

Bottom of the World (p. 3)

Critical Thinking — Fact or Opinion?

A *fact* can be proven. An *opinion* is a belief. Opinions cannot be proven. Write *F* before each statement that is a fact. Write *O* before each statement that is an opinion.

_____ **1.** It was right of Amundsen to keep his plans a secret.

_____ **2.** Amundsen left Norway in the summer of 1910.

_____ **3.** Johansen should not have questioned Amundsen's decisions.

_____ **4.** It was wrong of Amundsen to rush his men.

_____ **5.** Amundsen and his men reached the South Pole.

Exploring Words

Read each sentence. Fill in the circle next to the best meaning for the word in dark print. If you need help, use a dictionary.

1. Amundsen and his men wanted to bring **glory** to themselves and to Norway.
   ⓐ money   ⓑ great honor   ⓒ blame

2. The journey to the South Pole was **incredibly** difficult.
   ⓐ only a little   ⓑ usually   ⓒ in a way that is hard to believe

3. Amundsen didn't always make good **decisions**.
   ⓐ fires   ⓑ a kind of food   ⓒ what he decided to do

4. The men **struggled** in the cold weather.
   ⓐ worked hard   ⓑ laughed   ⓒ fought

5. Amundsen didn't want to **risk** letting Scott get ahead of him.
   ⓐ tell about   ⓑ think about   ⓒ take a chance on

6. Although the weather got warmer, it was a **false** spring.
   ⓐ late   ⓑ not real   ⓒ pretty

7. One of Amundsen's men thought he saw Scott, but it was just his **imagination**.
   ⓐ mind making things up ⓑ friend   ⓒ bad eyes

8. Their **goal** was to reach the South Pole.
   ⓐ fear   ⓑ what they were trying to do   ⓒ what they were avoiding

Life in the Wild

Jane Goodall lay in her tent near Kenya's Lake Tanganyika. Her face was covered with sweat and her body shook. Her temperature was 104 degrees. Next to her lay her mother, Vanne Goodall. Like Jane, Vanne had caught malaria. Her fever was 105 degrees.

"This fever will never end," whispered Vanne weakly.

"But it has to end," said Jane. "I have to get back to work. I have to keep looking for the chimps."

Jane Goodall and her mother, Vanne, had been in Kenya for two months. Jane had come to study wild chimpanzees. African officials would not let her live out in the wilderness alone, so Jane's mother had come with her. Jane was only 26 years old and had never studied wild animals before. Yet she hoped to do what no one else had ever done. She hoped to learn the secrets of chimpanzee behavior.

"There is so much people don't know," Jane thought. "Do chimps live alone or in groups? Do they eat meat? How do they care for their babies? Do they ever get into fights?"

Jane hoped to answer these questions. Every day she walked through the forest looking for chimpanzees. She had to be careful; the thick trees hid many dangers. Leopards and buffalo might attack if they were startled. Jane moved cautiously. She tried not to scare any of the animals. Often she heard the "hoos" of nearby chimpanzees and sometimes she caught sight of a chimpanzee, but it always ran away from her. After two months, Jane was discouraged.

"Am I ever going to make any progress?" she wondered sadly.

Then came the malaria. Jane and her mother both grew terribly ill. For a few days they feared they would die. At last, however, their fevers broke, and Jane returned to the forest in search of the chimps.

This time she got lucky. She found a group of chimps eating figs from a fig tree. She expected the chimps to run away in fear, but they didn't. In fact, they came closer and closer. Soon they were only 80 yards away. Jane was very excited, but she forced herself to be quiet. All day she stood still, watching the chimps. That night she raced back to her tent to tell her mother of her discovery. Then she took out some paper and wrote down everything she had seen.

From that day on, Jane made steady progress. Soon she could tell the chimps apart. She gave them each a name to keep track of them. She watched the way these chimps lived. She watched them walk, sleep, and climb. She wanted to learn all she could about them. So she began to try their food. When they ate

Life in the Wild (p. 2)

termites, she ate termites; when they ate ants, she ate ants.

Jane also watched the way chimps treated each other. She saw them play and groom each other, she saw mother chimps feeding their babies, and she saw male chimps fight each other for control of the group.

After a few months in Kenya, Vanne Goodall decided it was time to go home. She packed her bags and returned to England. Jane hated to see her go. She was lonely without her mother, but she had the chimps to keep her company, and she had her work to keep her busy.

As Jane spent time with the chimps, they slowly lost their fear of her. After eight months, she could come within 50 yards of them. After 14 months, the distance dropped to ten yards. And finally, after 18 months, a chimpanzee walked right into Jane's camp. That was

when she knew for sure she had earned the chimps' trust.

For over 20 years, Jane Goodall worked in Kenya. She learned many amazing things. She learned that chimps in the wild are very much like people. They eat meat and use tools. They feel many of the same emotions that humans do. Jane Goodall's work has shown that humans and chimpanzees are not so different after all.

Critical Thinking — Drawing Conclusions

Finish each sentence by writing the best answer.

1. Jane's mother, Vanne, came with her to Kenya because _____
_____.

2. Jane came to Kenya to study chimpanzees because _____
_____.

3. Jane had to be careful in the forest because _____
_____.

4. Jane tried eating the chimps' food because _____
_____.

Name _____   Date _____

Life in the Wild (p. 3)

Do You Remember?

In the blank, write the letter of the best ending for each sentence.

_____ **1.** Vanne Goodall was Jane's
   a. mother.   b. sister.   c. daughter.

_____ **2.** Jane Goodall began studying chimps when she was
   a. 16 years old.   b. 26 years old.   c. 46 years old.

_____ **3.** Jane went to Kenya to study chimps in the
   a. zoo.   b. desert.   c. forest.

_____ **4.** Jane and her mother were both sick with
   a. malaria.   b. the flu.   c. colds.

_____ **5.** Jane learned that chimpanzees are very much like
   a. cats.   b. dogs.   c. people.

Exploring Words

Use the words in the box to complete the paragraphs. Reread the paragraphs to be sure they make sense.

male	progress	discouraged	fever	sweat
figs	emotions	malaria	officials	groom

Jane Goodall went to Kenya to study chimpanzees. African **(1)** _____ let her set up camp near Lake Tanganyika. She became **(2)** _____ when she felt she was making no **(3)** _____. Then she came down with a disease called **(4)** _____. She had a high **(5)** _____. Her face was covered with **(6)** _____.

When she was well again, Jane returned to her study of chimps. Slowly she earned their trust. She saw chimps eating **(7)** _____ from trees. Later she watched them **(8)** _____ each other. She also saw **(9)** _____ chimps fighting each other. Jane learned that they have many of the same **(10)** _____ as people.

     Stories of Challenge
Nonfiction 5, SV 6180-X

Skiing Down Everest

Yuichiro Miura, a Japanese speed skier, raced down the snowy slope at Cervinia, Italy. He reached a speed of 107 miles per hour. "I can do it," he thought. "I can win this race. If I do, I'll become the speed-skiing champion of the world." But suddenly Miura lost control. He fell down the steep slope. After tumbling hundreds of yards, he stopped. Somehow he managed to get to his feet again.

Bravely Miura went on with the race. He fell two more times. Both times he was going over 105 miles per hour. In the end, he finished sixth, but skiing at Cervinia had given him an idea.

"I need to develop a good braking system," he thought. "Then I can push speed skiing to new levels." He decided there was only one safe way to brake at such high speeds; he would use a parachute. No one had ever tried this, but Miura believed it would work. In 1967, Miura decided to try his plan on Mount Fuji, in Japan. Boldly he climbed up this 12,388-foot-tall mountain. He strapped on his skis, buckled a parachute onto his back, and then hurled himself down the side of the mountain. It worked! When he opened the parachute, he slowed down. He was able to ski safely down the mountain.

Shortly after that, Miura began looking for a higher mountain with a steeper slope. A friend suggested Everest.

Others laughed when they heard that idea. Mt. Everest is the tallest mountain in the world. It is in Nepal, a country between India and China, and stands 29,028 feet tall. Many people have died just trying to climb it. Surely no one would try to ski down its deadly slopes. But Miura was excited. To him, this sounded like the greatest challenge of all.

Miura trained a long time for his trip to Mount Everest. He ran hundreds of miles, skied icy trails, and swam in freezing water. In the spring of 1970, he flew to Nepal and began the 100-mile climb to the Mt. Everest Base Camp. With him went 800 workers and several Japanese friends.

Each day the group climbed higher. At high altitudes, there is not much oxygen in the air. People become weak and sometimes get altitude sickness, which makes them sick to their stomachs and makes it difficult for them to breathe. High altitude can also cause heart attacks. As Miura climbed, he thought of all these things, but he refused to be afraid.

In early April, Miura reached 18,000 feet. He stopped there for two weeks to get used to skiing at such high altitudes. While he was there, some people in the group were caught in an ice slide. Ice on the side of the mountain suddenly gave way and dropped down into a deep hole. Six of Miura's guides were carried down with it and were killed instantly. Everyone in the group was deeply saddened. Some wanted to quit and go home, but Miura kept going. He planned to ski down Mt. Everest or die trying.

On May 7, 1970, Miura reached an altitude of 26,516 feet. Here, at last, was

Skiing Down Everest (p. 2)

the South Col. This long, steep slope on the south side of the mountain was 8,000 feet long and covered with hard ice. There were many rocks sticking up out of the ice. Miura planned to ski down the entire length of South Col.

At the bottom of the long slope was a huge cliff. If Miura fell over this cliff, he would die. He had to stop before he got there. Miura stood sideways on the slope of South Col. He put on his parachute and oxygen mask. Then he leaned over to strap on his skis. The slope was so steep that his shoulder bumped against the icy trail above him.

Miura stared down the mountain for a moment. "In about six seconds my speed should reach between 110 and 125 miles per hour," he thought. "The edges of my skis can't possibly help me stop on this ice. The parachute is my only chance."

With one quick motion, Miura turned and began skiing down the slope. His skis bounced on the ice, and his legs shook. He managed to stay in control and pulled the cord on his parachute. It opened, but in

the high, thin air, it did not hold him back; instead, it just dragged along behind him. Miura tried to brake with his skis, but the edges could not cut into the hard ice. In just two minutes, he covered 6,000 feet.

"My braking is hopeless," he thought wildly. "I am moving far too fast."

Then his skis hit something and he fell. He slid toward the cliff at a frightening speed. He was just seconds away from death. Then, suddenly, he crashed into a large rock and was knocked out.

When Miura awoke, he could hardly believe that he was still alive. But he was, and he was not hurt! He was lying just a few yards from the edge of the cliff. As he lay there, his heart filled with joy. He had done it! He had become the first person ever to ski down Mt. Everest.

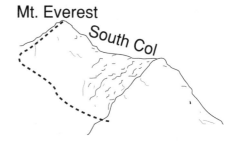

Mt. Everest

South Col

Do You Remember?

In the blank, write the letter of the best ending for each sentence.

_____ **1.** Yuichiro Miura's new braking system used
     a. weights.   b. parachutes.   c. ski poles.

_____ **2.** High altitude can hurt a person's
     a. bones.   b. eyes.   c. heart.

_____ **3.** While climbing up Mt. Everest, six of Miura's guides
     a. died.   b. lost their way.   c. broke their skis.

_____ **4.** At the bottom of South Col was a
     a. cabin.   b. fence.   c. cliff.

Stories of Challenge
Nonfiction 5, SV 6180-X

Skiing Down Everest (p. 3)

Express Yourself

Pretend you are Yuichiro Miura. You are planning to ski down Mount Everest. Some of your friends think it is a dangerous and foolish idea. On a separate piece of paper, write a letter to one of these friends explaining why you want to ski down Everest.

Exploring Words

Use the clues to complete the puzzle. Choose from the words in the box.

miles per hour
braking
system
hurled
deadly
altitudes
oxygen
entire
sideways
death

Across
3. a way of measuring speed
7. the end of life
8. whole
9. able to kill
10. one of the gases in air

Down
1. threw
2. stopping
4. with the side in front
5. high places
6. a group of parts that work together

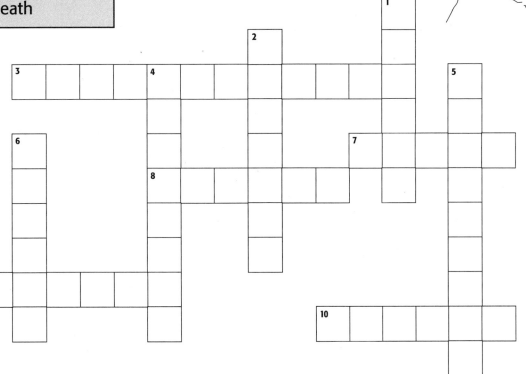

A Ship in Flames

The French ship, *Vinh-Long*, was sailing off the coast of Turkey. An officer on board smoked a cigarette as he kept watch. It was almost dawn, and he was tired. As he left the deck, he dropped his cigarette. It landed near some trash.

Within moments, a fire had started. The flames crept toward a leaking gasoline drum. Suddenly, fire shot into the air. A great explosion followed. The *Vinh-Long* carried a large amount of gunpowder. If the fire set it off, there would be no hope. The huge French ship would explode, and all 500 people aboard would be killed.

The fire broke out on December 16, 1922. Three miles away from the *Vinh-Long* sailed a tiny American ship—the *Bainbridge*. An officer on the *Bainbridge* saw the flash of fire. He sent for Captain W. A. Edwards.

When Edwards saw the flames, he sounded an alarm. Sailors dashed to their stations. They grabbed fire and rescue equipment. Then they lined up by the lifeboats. They were ready for action. Edwards smiled; he knew he had a good crew.

Soon the *Bainbridge* reached the *Vinh-Long*. Edwards yelled out, "Ship ahoy! Can we be of assistance?"

The French captain was about to answer when another blast shook the *Vinh-Long*.

Edwards later said, "His ship answered for him. A terrific roar deafened us. The middle of his ship had blown up. I knew a dreadful experience lay ahead."

The force of the blast had blown people into the water. Screams of frightened people filled the night. The *Bainbridge* sailors rowed out into the dark waters. They lifted people out of the water as fast as they could.

One of the people rescued was a French sailor. He was half out of his mind with fear. "She's loaded with gunpowder," he screamed. "She will blow up in a moment! You will be blown up, too!"

Captain Edwards stopped to think. His ship also carried explosives. One well-placed spark and his ship would be blazing just like the *Vinh-Long*.

Edwards said later, "I wanted to help the people on the blazing ship. But I could not forget that I had nearly 100 fine young Americans on my own ship. They were ready to obey my every order. The sight of dying men did not make them flinch. But I flinched when I thought of asking them to do what seemed the only right and decent thing to do."

The captain didn't want to put his men in danger, but he had to do something. He brought his ship next to the *Vinh-Long*. The people on the *Vinh-Long* crowded against the rail, ready to jump onto the *Bainbridge*. They knew the huge ship could blow up at any moment.

Just then came the worst explosion yet. People on both ships were knocked

A Ship in Flames (p. 2)

off their feet; everyone was blinded for a moment. The force of the blast pushed the *Bainbridge* away from the *Vinh-Long*.

Edwards knew he had to try something else. He would ram the French ship. He hoped this would damage the *Vinh-Long's* hull. Then water would rush in and slow down the fire. If his plan worked, the people on board would have time to get off. If it didn't work, both ships might explode.

Edwards gave the order, and the *Bainbridge* rammed into the *Vinh-Long* with perfect aim. The flaming ship's hull broke open. The people on board went wild. They knew that every second counted. They poured onto the *Bainbridge*. Soon everyone who was still alive was on the American ship.

Edwards ordered his ship to move away. The *Bainbridge* pulled free. The

rescue was complete! Edwards and his crew had saved 482 people. President Coolidge later presented Captain Edwards with the Medal of Honor for his bravery.

Do You Remember?

In the blank, write the letter of the best ending for each sentence.

_____ **1.** The *Bainbridge* was a
   a. big French ship.   b. small U.S. ship.   c. lifeboat.

_____ **2.** The fire was started by
   a. lightning.   b. W. A. Edwards.   c. a cigarette.

_____ **3.** The *Vinh-Long* carried
   a. gunpowder.   b. no passengers.   c. circus animals.

_____ **4.** Some people got off the *Vinh-Long* by jumping onto
   a. helicopters.   b. the *Bainbridge*.   c. gasoline tanks.

_____ **5.** The *Bainbridge* finally
   a. sank.   b. blew up.   c. crashed into the *Vinh-Long*.

Name _____   Date _____

A Ship in Flames (p. 3)

Express Yourself

Imagine you are a crew member of the *Bainbridge*. On a separate piece of paper, write a letter to a friend about your experience with the rescue of the *Vinh-Long*.

Exploring Words

Choose the correct word from the box to complete each sentence.

cigarette	explosion	equipment	assistance	dreadful
experience	explosives	flinch	ram	hull

1. The sailors grabbed fire and rescue _____.

2. When you help someone, you give _____.

3. A _____ is a roll of tobacco that is wrapped in paper and smoked.

4. When the gunpowder caught on fire, there was a great _____.

5. The body of a ship is called the _____.

6. Something that is _____ is very bad.

7. Materials used to blow something up are called _____.

8. If you _____, it means that you back away from danger.

9. An _____ is something you see, do, or live through.

10. To run into something with great force is to _____ it.

© Steck-Vaughn Company

Nonfiction 5, SV 6180-X

Do or Die!

"Fire!"

Early in the morning on June 13, 1982, Karen Hartsock stirred in her bed. She thought she heard her father's voice. A few seconds passed, and she heard it again.

"Fire! Fire!"

This time Karen was wide awake. She wasn't having a dream; the house was on fire!

Fourteen-year-old Karen jumped out of bed. She ran from her second-floor bedroom into the hall. Fire and smoke were everywhere. Flames covered the floor and the walls. Karen was frightened. Her parents were downstairs where they could escape, but what about her younger brother and sisters? Karen yelled to them.

Eleven-year-old Norma ran crying from her room. Karen grabbed her hand and ran for the stairs. The stairs were on fire, but this was the only path to safety. Karen pulled Norma through the flames and pushed her toward her father. Mr. Hartsock was quite weak from a recent heart operation, but he put out the flames on Norma's pajamas as quickly as he could.

Karen's 12-year-old sister, Loretta, was still upstairs. So was 9-year-old Johnny. Karen would not leave the house without them. She was especially worried about Johnny. He had cerebral palsy and couldn't get out of the house by himself.

Karen raced back up the blazing stairs. As she did, her nightgown burst into flames.

"Help me!" she cried out in pain.

Fire burned her back and legs. The pain was terrible, but she did not turn back. She dashed into Johnny's room, and saw her little brother still asleep in his bed. Quickly, Karen wrapped Johnny in a blanket. She picked him up and ran back toward the stairs. Burning wallpaper fell on her arms and shoulders, and her hair caught on fire. With one arm, she held Johnny; with the other, she tried to put out the fire in her hair.

Karen didn't think she could stand the pain. Then suddenly she couldn't feel anything. The fire had burned deep into her skin and had damaged her nerves. She almost felt normal again. At the bottom of the stairs, Karen saw her father.

"Here!" she shouted, throwing Johnny to him.

"I've got him! Now you come on! Come on!" begged her father.

But Karen ran back up the burning stairs. She didn't know it at the time, but Loretta had already gotten out of the house. Suddenly, the stairs collapsed and Karen was buried in a pile of burning wood. Using all his strength, Mr. Hartsock pulled Karen out of the house. Then Mrs. Hartsock threw herself on Karen to put out the flames. Karen struggled to get up. She still thought Loretta needed her help. The family held Karen down while fire swallowed up the house. Karen was so badly burned it seemed certain she would die.

After several minutes, an ambulance

Do or Die! (p. 2)

arrived and rushed Karen to the hospital. The doctors said Karen had only a ten percent chance of living. Her burns were deep and covered most of her body.

The doctors worked hard to save her. They put a tube in her throat to help her breathe; they removed the burned skin and replaced it with healthy skin, and wrapped her in bandages. For many days, Karen clung to life. Her family begged her not to give up, and she didn't. Although the medicines made her sleepy, Karen struggled to stay awake. The treatments were painful, but she didn't complain.

One day Karen seemed very upset. She signaled and pointed. Finally, they figured out that Karen wanted to see Loretta. She was afraid Loretta had died in the fire. In a few minutes, Loretta was sitting beside her.

"Please get well, Big Sister. We're all so lonely without you," Loretta said. Karen beamed. She started to improve soon after that.

Finally, the danger passed. Karen would live, but her face and body were covered with thick scars. When the bandages were removed from her eyes, Karen was shocked. She had not realized how different she looked. She began crying. Slowly, Karen accepted her looks. She had many more operations in which the doctors were able to replace some of the scar tissue with healthy skin. After nine months, Karen was released from the hospital. She was very happy to go home.

In July 1983, Karen won the Young American Medal for Bravery. She also won the Carnegie Medal for heroism. But Karen didn't see herself as a hero.

She said, "When you love the people in your family, you will do anything for them. That night I saw they were upstairs. I knew I loved them. I couldn't let them die. So I went back and back again for them. If you love somebody, you can do things you never dreamed you could do."

Do You Remember?

Read each sentence below. Write _T_ if the sentence is true. Write _F_ if the sentence is false.

_____ **1.** Karen's sister Loretta was killed in the fire.

_____ **2.** Karen saved her brother, Johnny.

_____ **3.** Karen's hair caught on fire.

_____ **4.** Mr. Hartsock begged Karen to rescue Loretta.

_____ **5.** Doctors were not hopeful about Karen's chances of living.

Stories of Rescue

Do or Die! (p. 3)

Critical Thinking — Main Ideas

Underline the two most important ideas from the story.

1. An ambulance rushed Karen Hartsock to the hospital.

2. Karen wrapped Johnny in a blanket.

3. Karen Hartsock risked her life to save her brother and sisters.

4. Karen lived even though doctors did not think she would.

Exploring Words

Use the clues to complete the puzzle. Choose from the words in the box.

especially
cerebral palsy
treatment
ambulance
percent
clung
operation
scars
tissue
heroism

Across
2. a layer of cells
4. marks caused by injuries
6. courage
7. medical care given
9. a muscle disease
10. parts in each 100

Down
1. something done using instruments to repair an injury
3. a special way
5. takes people to the hospital
8. held on tightly

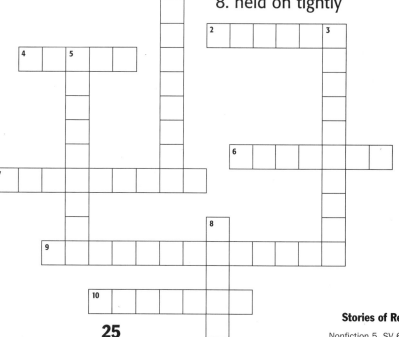

Abandon Ship!

"This is your captain speaking. There is a small fire in the engine room. It is under control. There is no cause for alarm. But for your own safety, please report to the upper deck."

That message came about 1 A.M. on the morning of October 4, 1980. Most of the 324 passengers were not worried. After all, the *Prinsendam* was a safe ship, so why should they panic? Some passengers took their life preservers, but others didn't bother; they went to the upper deck dressed in their pajamas.

The *Prinsendam* left Vancouver, Canada, on September 30. It was the beginning of a month-long  luxury cruise to Asia. Most of the passengers were 65 years old and older. Many had saved for years to take this trip. But after just three days at sea, disaster struck.

The trouble began 120 miles off the coast of Alaska. The fuel system started to leak. Oil from the engine spurted onto a hot pipe and burst into flames. Crew members sealed off the engine room. They tried to smother the flames, but the fire kept raging.

At 2:25 A.M., the *Prinsendam* sent out an SOS. Admiral School at the Coast Guard Center in Juneau, Alaska, received the message. He radioed officials in Kodiak Island, Anchorage, and British Columbia. Soon, helicopters were flying toward the *Prinsendam* from all directions.

The ship's SOS had also been heard by the *Williamsburgh*. The *Williamsburgh* was a huge oil tanker, 90 miles south of the *Prinsendam*. It turned around and sailed toward the troubled ship.

Meanwhile, the *Prinsendam* crew kept fighting the fire. They did the best they could, but at 4:54 A.M., Captain Cornelius Wabeke saw it was no use. He announced the news over the loudspeaker.

"I'm sorry. The fire is completely out of control. We have to abandon ship."

Getting the lifeboats loaded and into the water was not easy. The fire had cut off the ship's electricity. There were no lights. Finally, a helicopter arrived and pointed a bright light on the ship.

By 6:30 A.M., all the lifeboats and their passengers were lowered into the water. Captain Wabeke worried as he watched the lifeboats leave. He wondered how the older passengers would manage. Some of them had weak hearts, and a few were in wheelchairs. He hoped the sea would remain calm.

Luckily, the *Williamsburgh*, the huge oil tanker, had arrived. One of the lifeboats got next to the tanker, and someone dropped a rope ladder over the side.

One by one, the frightened passengers tried to climb the rope ladder, but it was a long 40-foot climb. It would take more than a full day to rescue all 524 people this way, and a storm was blowing in. The waves were getting higher and the other lifeboats were drifting away from

Stories of Rescue

Abandon Ship! (p. 2)

the *Williamsburgh*. Something else needed to be done.

More helicopters arrived. An order was given to lift people from the lifeboats onto the *Williamsburgh*. The pilots lowered one-person baskets to the lifeboats. The pilots had to keep their helicopters steady, but still baskets swung in the wind.

As a basket was lowered, someone grabbed it and crawled in. The passenger held on tightly as the basket was raised to the helicopter. Some people were so scared they kept their eyes shut.

When a helicopter was full, it would fly to the *Williamsburgh* where passengers would be unloaded. The helicopter would then return to pick up more people from the lifeboat. Crew members made the trip again and again.

Finally, by the next morning, the rescue was complete. All 524 people on board the *Prinsendam* had been saved, and none had been badly hurt. The largest sea rescue in history was a success.

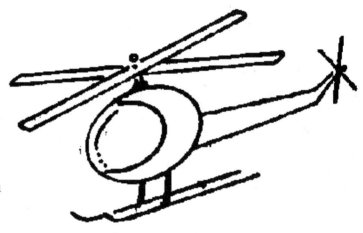

Do You Remember?

Read each sentence below. Write *T* if the sentence is true. Write *F* if the sentence is false.

_____ **1.** The *Prinsendam* was sailing to Asia.

_____ **2.** The *Prinsendam* sent out an SOS.

_____ **3.** Helicopters joined in the rescue effort.

_____ **4.** Passengers were rescued by motorboats.

_____ **5.** All 524 people on board were saved.

Abandon Ship! (p. 3)

Critical Thinking — Drawing Conclusions

Finish each sentence by writing the best answer.

1. The fire broke out because _____
_____.

2. The passengers were told to abandon ship because _____
_____.

3. The *Williamsburgh* turned around because _____
_____.

4. Captain Wabeke was worried about the passengers because _____
_____.

Exploring Words

Read each sentence. Fill in the circle next to the best meaning for the word in dark print. If you need help, use a dictionary.

1. People did not **panic** when they first heard about the fire.
ⓐ become frightened   ⓑ cheer   ⓒ listen

2. Oil from the engine **spurted** onto a hot pipe.
ⓐ shined   ⓑ poured out   ⓒ planted

3. The cruise turned into a **disaster**.
ⓐ mystery   ⓑ terrible failure   ⓒ great joke

4. The passengers had to **abandon** the ship.
ⓐ watch   ⓑ rock   ⓒ leave

5. An **admiral** was in charge of the rescue.
ⓐ police officer   ⓑ navy officer   ⓒ principal

Trapped in a Well

Reba McClure stood in the bright Texas sunshine. She smiled at the children playing in the backyard. One of them was her own 18-month-old Jessica.

Just then, at 9:30 A.M. on October 14, 1987, the phone rang. Reba was gone only a few minutes, but when she returned, the children were no longer playing. They were gathered around an eight-inch hole in the ground.

Reba did not see Jessica. Her heart began to pound. That was when the nightmare began. Jessica had fallen into an old, dry well. The 17-year-old Reba became terrified. She ran inside and called the police. Three minutes later, the police arrived. Officer B. J. Hall tried to calm Reba down.

"We won't let her die," he said. But Hall was not sure he could keep that promise. Jessica was trapped about 22 feet underground in a space that was only 12 inches wide. Hall didn't know if Jessica was badly hurt, if she had enough air to breathe, or even if she was still alive.

The officers dropped a microphone down the hole. They heard a sad little cry. She was alive! Hall quickly ordered some equipment so they could start digging the child out.

City workers rushed in with a backhoe. They planned to dig a second hole right next to Jessica 29 feet under the ground. Then they would dig a slanted tunnel up toward Jessica. They would break through the wall of the well about two feet below her and slide her into the new hole.

The workers dug down two feet. Then they hit solid rock. Bigger, heavier equipment was brought in. Their drill bits kept breaking, but they simply replaced them and kept on drilling. They stopped only to listen for Jessica's cries. As long as they heard her, they knew she was still alive.

Progress was slow. When darkness fell, the workers had only gone a few feet. New workers came in to continue the job. Meanwhile, Reba and her husband, Chip, clung to each other in fear.

By the next morning, drillers finally got the second hole deep enough. Then they began to dig the tunnel toward Jessica. This was the most difficult part of the job. It took an hour to drill through one inch of rock. A worker had to lie on his stomach while he drilled with a 45-pound jackhammer. Even the strongest person could only handle it for 30 or 40 minutes at a time.

"The jackhammer would bounce off the rock. It was like hitting a piece of steel," driller Paul Wilhite said. It was also frightening to be in such a small hole that far underground. Said Wilhite, "It was scary. It was like being in a grave."

One driller collapsed in the hole. He had to be carried up. Others had to leave when the dust and dirt choked them. But the workers weren't giving up. They could still hear Jessica. When she began

29 Nonfiction 5, SV 6180-X

Trapped in a Well (p. 2)

singing her favorite Winnie-the-Pooh song, their eyes filled with tears.

Another night came and went. Jessica had been in the hole 48 hours. She was weak and hungry. Her right foot was jammed up against her face. She hardly made a sound and workers feared she was dying. One police officer called down to her to see if she was still alert.

"How does a kitten go?" he asked. "Meow," came the faint reply.

By noon, they finally reached Jessica. But the tunnel was only a few inches wide. Rescue worker Robert O'Donnell could touch her, but he couldn't get her out. The drillers made the tunnel wider. At about 6 P.M., it was wide enough. O'Donnell went back down the hole.

"Come on, Juicy," he said, calling Jessica by her family nickname. "Just stay calm. I'm going to get you out."

Gently, O'Donnell pulled at Jessica, but she was stuck in the hole. He pulled her harder, and she began to cry. For two long hours he worked to free her. He put clear jelly on the walls of the hole to help move her. Slowly, inch by inch, he pulled her closer. Then he gave a final tug, and Jessica fell into his arms.

"You're out, Juicy," he whispered. O'Donnell strapped her to a board to protect her back, and she was pulled up. Friends and reporters who had gathered around the hole cheered. Jessica had survived over 58 hours in the dark well. Her forehead was bruised, and her right foot was damaged. But for all she had been through, she was in good shape.

Tears again filled the eyes of the workers who had struggled to free her, but this time they were tears of happiness.

Do You Remember?

In the blank, write the letter of the best ending for each sentence.

_____ **1.** Jessica fell into an old
　　　　a. house. 　　　　b. well. 　　　　c. car.

_____ **2.** The backhoe only dug down two feet before hitting
　　　　a. oil. 　　　　b. water. 　　　　c. rock.

_____ **3.** A police officer asked Jessica to make the sound of a
　　　　a. cow. 　　　　b. bear. 　　　　c. kitten.

_____ **4.** Workers helped make a second
　　　　a. hole. 　　　　b. drill. 　　　　c. jackhammer.

_____ **5.** Jessica's nickname was
　　　　a. Winnie the Pooh. 　b. Juicy. 　　　　c. Reba.

Trapped in a Well (p. 3)

Critical Thinking — Finding the Sequence ⚡

Number the sentences to show the order in which things happened in the story.

_____ Reba ran inside the house to answer the phone.

_____ Jessica was strapped to a board to protect her back.

_____ Police officers arrived on the scene.

_____ O'Donnell put clear jelly on the walls of the hole.

_____ The drill bits kept breaking.

Exploring Words 🔍

Use the words in the box to complete the paragraph. Reread the paragraph to be sure it makes sense.

nightmare	jackhammer	alert	progress
microphone	grave	drill bits	solid

Reba McClure discovered that little Jessica had fallen into

a deep hole. Police officers dropped a **(1)** _____

into the hole so that they could listen to the child. To dig

through the **(2)** _____ rock, workers also brought in a

(3) _____, but **(4)** _____ was slow. The **(5)** _____

on their machines kept breaking. As the tunnel got deeper, some of them felt as

if they were working in a **(6)** _____. At last, they reached Jessica.

She was frightened but **(7)** _____. After over 58 hours, the

(8) _____ was over.

Doctor Under Fire

"Goodbye!" Mary Walker called to her neighbor as she loaded her bags into a carriage.

The neighbor stared at Walker's suitcases and traveling clothes. "Where are you going?" he asked.

"I'm leaving New York," Walker told him. "I'm going to Washington. Now that the Civil War is on, the Union needs me."

"What are you talking about?" laughed the neighbor. "You're a woman. You can't be a soldier."

"I'm a doctor," Walker reminded him. "I can care for the wounded."

Walker arrived in Washington, D.C., in October 1861. She asked to become a surgeon in the Army. The United States government turned her down. Government leaders did not think women should be doctors. And they certainly did not think women belonged in the Army.

"I don't care what they think," Dr. Walker said to herself. "The soldiers need me."

With that, Walker marched into a soldiers' hospital in Washington. She found the man in charge. His name was Dr. J. N. Green. "I'm a doctor," she told Green. "I'm here to help you."

Dr. Green looked at Walker in surprise. At first he was not sure whether she was a man or a woman. In the 1860s, all women wore dresses. But Mary Walker was different. She wore men's pants. She found them to be more comfortable.

"I do need help," said Dr. Green after a minute. "We have so many injured men here, and more arrive every day."

That was all Walker needed to hear. For the next few months she served as a volunteer in the hospital. Day after day she cared for wounded soldiers. She dressed their cuts and changed their bandages. She gave them medicine for their pain. She comforted them as they were dying.

In 1862, Walker returned to New York to earn a second degree in medicine. Then she went back to Washington. This time she didn't stay in the city. She heard there were not enough doctors out in the field. So she decided to go out to the front lines herself.

On December 13, 1862, Walker was in Fredericksburg, Virginia. A huge battle was taking place there. When it was over, the Union had suffered a terrible blow. Over 10,000 Union soldiers had been hurt or killed. Walker worked all through the night to help the wounded.

In the fall of 1863, Walker went to a Union camp in Tennessee. There she saw that soldiers were not the only ones suffering. All over the South, women, children, and old people needed medical help. Doctors were too busy with wounded soldiers to care for these people.

"We have to do something," Walker said to the other Union doctors. "These people need our help."

"But they are the enemy!" the doctors told her. "We cannot care for them. They are Confederates."

"They may be Confederates, but

Doctor Under Fire (p. 2)

they're still human beings. And they're suffering! They need help. If you won't give it to them, I will!"

With that, Walker packed up her supplies. She climbed onto a horse and rode out into the countryside. She went from house to house, visiting the sick. Every day she made trips to Confederate homes to offer help and hand out medicine. She knew it was dangerous work. She knew that at any minute she might be captured or killed. But that was a chance she was willing to take.

On April 10, 1864, it finally happened. As Walker rode down a dirt path, Confederate soldiers sprang out of the woods. They arrested her and took her away. For four months she was locked in a crowded Southern prison. At last, in August 1864, she was set free.

After getting out of prison, Walker was made an Assistant Surgeon in the United States Army. She was the first woman ever to hold this post. For Mary Walker, this meant a great deal. She was proud to be part of the United States Army. She was also proud to show that women could be useful doctors.

After the war, Walker was given the Congressional Medal of Honor. It was the first time a woman had received this honor. Walker was thrilled. She had earned a place in the Army. And she had earned a place in history.

Critical Thinking - Cause and Effect

Complete the following sentences.

1. Mary Walker went to Washington, D.C., during the Civil War because _____

_____.

2. Walker decided to go out to the front lines because _____

_____.

3. Southern doctors did not care for Southern women and children because _____

_____.

4. Walker made trips to Confederate homes because _____

_____.

33   **Stories of Firsts**

Nonfiction 5, SV 6180-X

Doctor Under Fire (p. 3)

Do You Remember?

Write *T* if the sentence is true. Write *F* if the sentence is false.

_____ **1.** Government leaders did not think women should be doctors.

_____ **2.** Walker worked with Dr. J. N. Green as a volunteer.

_____ **3.** Walker didn't finish earning her second degree in medicine.

_____ **4.** Walker refused to work on the front lines.

_____ **5.** A huge battle took place in Fredericksburg, Virginia.

Exploring Words

Read each sentence. Fill in the circle next to the best meaning for the word in dark print. You may use a dictionary.

1. Mary Walker believed the **Union** needed her.
- ⓐ a rock group
- ⓑ what the United States was called during the Civil War
- ⓒ women's club

2. Walker knew she could help the **wounded**.
- ⓐ those hurt in battle
- ⓑ tired people
- ⓒ confused people

3. She asked to become a **surgeon** in the Army.
- ⓐ soldier
- ⓑ leader
- ⓒ doctor

4. Dr. Green had to care for many **injured** men.
- ⓐ lonely
- ⓑ hurt
- ⓒ old

5. She **dressed** soldiers' wounds.
- ⓐ sewed up
- ⓑ cleaned and bandaged
- ⓒ clothed

6. She decided to go out to the **front lines** herself.
- ⓐ where the fighting is
- ⓑ seashore
- ⓒ newspaper office

7. Walker wanted to care for **Confederate** women and children.
- ⓐ poor
- ⓑ homeless
- ⓒ Southern

8. Walker was given the **Congressional** Medal of Honor.
- ⓐ special
- ⓑ from the U.S. Congress
- ⓒ gold

Reaching for the Sky

Five-year-old Jacqueline Cochran walked along a beach in northern Florida. She shivered in the damp air.

"No food today," she thought sadly as she sat down near the water. Jackie, as she was called, often came to this beach looking for food. She searched for crabs or fish or anything else to eat. Her foster parents were very poor. On this day in 1915, Jackie's stomach ached from hunger. Brushing a tear from her eye, she saw a bird fly overheard.

"I wish I could fly like that bird!" she thought suddenly. "I wish I could just fly away from here!"

Unfortunately, little Jackie was trapped in a life of dirt and hunger. When she was six, her foster parents moved to Georgia. Jackie slept on the floor of a small hut. She had no shoes, no dress, no winter coat. Once she got so hungry that she stole pig food from a farmer.

Jackie and her parents moved to Bagdad, Florida. One day Jackie showed up at the small schoolhouse there. She thought the teacher, Miss Bostwick, seemed nice, so she stayed for class. "Miss Bostwick taught me how to keep my body and clothes clean and how to comb my hair," Jackie later wrote. "She taught me to read. She lifted the horizons for me and gave me ambition."

After two years, Miss Bostwick moved north, and Jackie quit going to school. But because of Miss Bostwick, Jackie had new hopes and dreams.

When she was just eight years old, Jackie went to work in a cotton mill. She worked all night, from 6 P.M. to 6 A.M. The mill was hot and dirty. The lighting was awful. There was no place to sit down, no place to eat, and there were no bathrooms. Still, Jackie felt lucky to have the job.

"I'm on my way," she told herself. "I'm going to save my money and get myself out of this place."

When Jackie was ten, she moved away from home and got a job working in a beauty shop. She learned to cut, curl, and color hair. By working hard and spending little, Jackie saved some money. At the age of 20, she moved to New York. There she got a job in a fancy beauty shop. In many ways Jackie was a success, but she wasn't really happy. She decided to become a traveling salesperson. She planned to sell beauty creams from coast to coast.

A friend said, "I don't know, Jackie. The competition out there is pretty tough. You'd almost need wings to cover all the area you're talking about."

Jackie laughed. But the words stuck in her head. Soon after that, Jackie showed up at the Roosevelt Field Flying School in Long Island, New York. She told the people there, "I want to become a pilot."

Jackie was told that it took two months to become a pilot. "I can do it in three weeks," she announced. For the next three weeks, she spent all her time at the airfield. Before the third week ended, Jacqueline Cochran passed her pilot's test.

Reaching for the Sky (p. 2)

Jackie was thrilled. She still didn't know much about flying. She didn't know how to fly in clouds, or how to read air maps. She didn't even know how to use a compass. But flying had become the love of her life. She loved to soar with the birds and race with the wind. Over time, Jackie became a fine pilot. She won several important air races. She came close to death many times. But the joy of flying was worth all the dangers.

By 1953, the newest and latest planes had jet engines. Jackie was eager to fly one of these new jets. But at that time, all jet planes belonged to the United States government. Although Jackie was a member of the Air Force Reserve, government rules did not allow a woman to fly a jet. Jackie turned to the Canadian government. She asked to use one of their jet planes. In May 1953, she climbed into a Canadian Sabre jet. As she took off, she had a secret plan in mind. She wanted to be the first woman to break the sound barrier. This meant flying at Mach 1, or about 600 miles an hour. In other words, it meant flying faster than the speed of sound.

Jackie took the plane to 45,000 feet. Then she began diving straight for the ground. The wings of the plane rattled. The nose shook. Then Jackie felt a sudden shock wave. At that instant, she knew she had done it; she was moving faster than the speed of sound.

Jackie went on to break many other flying records. In 1953, she broke the men's and women's record for speed. In 1960, she became the first woman to hit Mach 2, or twice the speed of sound. In 1961, she set a world record for altitude. And in 1962, she became the first woman to fly a jet across the Atlantic Ocean.

As Jackie looked back over her life, she had to smile. She had overcome all the hardships of her early life. She was living proof that no dream is impossible.

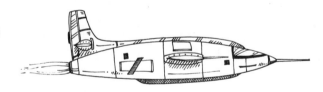

Express Yourself

Pretend you are Jackie Cochran. You have been asked to give a speech to children at a nearby school. What would you say? Write your speech on a separate piece of paper.

Reaching for the Sky (p. 3)

Do You Remember?

In the blank, write the letter of the best ending for each sentence.

_____ **1.** Jackie's foster parents were very
   a. happy.   b. rich.   c. poor.

_____ **2.** Jackie went to school for
   a. twelve years.   b. two years.   c. one day.

_____ **3.** When she was eight years old, Jackie went to work in a
   a. cotton mill.   b. beauty shop.   c. restaurant.

_____ **4.** Jackie took lessons to learn to
   a. fix cars.   b. sail.   c. fly.

_____ **5.** Jackie won several
   a. air races.   b. card games.   c. beauty contests.

Exploring Words

Use the words in the box to complete the paragraphs. Reread the paragraphs to be sure they make sense.

horizons	competition	altitude	hardships
compass	shock wave	ambition	

Jackie Cochran faced many **(1)** _____ as a child. A teacher named

Miss Bostwick taught Jackie to read. She widened

Jackie's **(2)** _____ and gave her

(3) _____.

As a young woman, Jackie wanted to sell makeup. There was a lot of

(4) _____ in this business. Jackie learned to fly so she could cover

more area. Jackie passed her pilot's test before she even learned to read a

(5) _____. In 1953, she wanted to break the sound barrier. She flew a

jet to an **(6)** _____ of 45,000 feet. Then she dived toward the ground.

She knew she had reached Mach 1 when she felt a **(7)** _____.

Stories of Firsts

Running for the Gold

Joan Benoit ran down the road in Freeport, Maine. She ran swiftly and easily.

Her feet pounded out a happy rhythm as she finished the 14th mile of this 20-mile run. Benoit loved to run. On this day, March 16, 1984, her mind was clear. Her body felt strong. Everything was going beautifully. And then it happened.

She felt something catch in her right knee. A sharp pain shot through the outside of the knee. Benoit slowed down. She hoped the pain would go away, but it didn't. Within a mile, she knew something was seriously wrong.

Benoit went to see a doctor who tried different treatments for her knee. Nothing worked. At last, on April 25, she had surgery. She hoped that would correct the problem. The surgery was a success. Within days, Benoit's knee felt healthy again. "Great!" she thought. "I can run again!"

Benoit was in a hurry to get back to training. The 1984 Summer Olympics in Los Angeles, California, were only three months away. There, 50 women from around the world would be running in a marathon, or 26-mile race. It would be the first time that the women's marathon would be part of the Olympic Games. Benoit wanted to win it. She wanted to win for herself, and she wanted to win for the United States.

"I know I can do it," she kept telling herself.

After all, Benoit held the record for the fastest women's marathon ever. Still, she would face tough competition in the Olympics. Grete Waitz from Norway would be running against her. Benoit and Waitz had run against each other in eleven races. Waitz had won ten of them.

Benoit had other worries, too. The race would be in Southern California. The temperature there might be 80 degrees or higher. Such heat could sap Benoit's strength. Then Rosa Mota from Portugal would have a better chance of winning. Mota loved hot weather.

On the morning of August 5, Benoit lined up at the starting point at Corsair Field in Santa Monica, California. It was already 68 degrees. The sun was hidden in the clouds, but Benoit knew the clouds would soon be gone. Then she would be running under the bright California sun. The crowd was silent while everyone waited for the starter's gun to sound.

"It's going to be hot," one runner said.

Benoit nodded. She looked nervously at the other runners. "I wonder how many of them like to run in the heat?" she asked herself.

At the sound of the gun, Benoit moved into the lead group. There were about 30 runners with her. Among them were Waitz and Mota. These women were running a mile every 5 minutes and 40 seconds. They looked comfortable. They had settled into a pace they liked. Benoit, however, felt edgy.

"This pace is too slow," she thought. "Everyone is holding back."

Benoit knew why. None of the runners

Running for the Gold (p. 2)

wanted to use up her energy too quickly. They all wanted to have some strength left for the final stretch. Benoit understood that. But her body was telling her to move faster. Her natural rhythm was quicker than the current pace.

In the third mile, Benoit began running faster. Soon she was 20 yards ahead of the others. As she started the fourth mile, she looked back over her shoulder. No one was trying to catch her.

"Am I making a mistake?" Benoit wondered. She knew that she would feel foolish if she led for half the race, and then everyone passed her.

She thought about slowing down, but she liked the quicker pace. "Forget what the others are doing," she told herself. "Just run your own race."

And so she did. By the fifth mile she had a 13-second lead over the others. After 10 miles, her lead was over a minute. In the 15th mile, Waitz and Mota finally made their move. They picked up

their pace and attempted to catch Benoit. But it was too late. Benoit's lead was enormous. After 19 miles she led by two full minutes. Waitz struggled to speed up in the hot sun. She forced herself to go faster. But she couldn't go fast enough. Even Mota, who liked the heat, couldn't catch Benoit.

With three miles to go, Benoit still had a 90-second lead. As she ran through the streets of Los Angeles, thousands of people cheered her on. Nearing the finish, she was the only runner in sight. When she crossed the finish line at the Los Angeles Memorial Coliseum, she felt a burst of joy. She had won! She was the best woman marathon runner in the world. And now she had the gold medal to prove it.

Do You Remember?

Write T if the sentence is true. Write F if the sentence is false.

_____ **1.** Benoit had surgery on her knee.

_____ **2.** Grete Waitz was a runner from Norway.

_____ **3.** The first Olympic marathon for women was held on a very cold day.

_____ **4.** During the first part of the Olympic race, Benoit thought the pace was too fast.

_____ **5.** Benoit led most of the way in the Olympic marathon.

Running for the Gold (p. 3)

Critical Thinking — Finding the Sequence

Number the sentences to show the order in which things happened in the story.

_____ Benoit hurt her knee.

_____ The runners gathered at Corsair Field in Santa Monica.

_____ Waitz and Mota attempted to catch Benoit.

_____ Benoit pulled ahead of the other runners.

_____ Benoit went to see a doctor.

Exploring Words

Use the words in the box to complete the paragraphs. Reread the paragraphs to be sure they make sense.

enormous	natural	pace	rhythm
current	seriously	surgery	edgy

Runner Joan Benoit knew there was something **(1)** _____

wrong with her knee. A doctor performed **(2)** _____.

After that, she was able to run with her regular, happy

(3) _____.

On August 5, 1984, Benoit ran a 26-mile Olympic race. In the first

two miles of the race, Benoit felt **(4)** _____. She didn't

like the **(5)** _____ speed of the race. It didn't seem

(6) _____ to her to be running so slowly. She pulled ahead of the others

and set her own **(7)** _____. Soon her lead was **(8)** _____.

She went on to win the race and earn a gold medal.

Race Across Alaska

Libby Riddles stepped onto the back of her dog sled. The crowd cheered as she waited for the signal. Finally it came. She whistled to her team of 15 dogs, and they set out across the snow.

She was heading out on the famous 1,172-mile Iditarod Trail Sled Dog Race. It went from Anchorage, Alaska, to Nome, Alaska. Riddles knew it would be a grueling race. For two weeks she would battle blizzards, cold weather, and angry moose. Still, Riddles hoped to be the first woman ever to win the Iditarod.

Libby Riddles was born in Wisconsin. When she was 16, she moved to Alaska. There she became interested in dogsled racing. She watched racers and learned how to work with dogs. Later, she raised her own sled dogs.

Riddles had entered the Iditarod before, but this time she was out to win. As Riddles pulled out of Anchorage, she checked the time. It was 11:30 A.M. on March 3, 1985. She felt great. The weather was fairly warm for Alaska; it was over 20 degrees. Her dogs were healthy and strong.

In the first few days, Riddles made good time. She often drove 14 or more hours without resting. She did stop often to feed her dogs. Libby always fed her dogs before she fed herself. To keep them strong, she fed them beef, chicken, lamb, and seal meat cooked in a hot gravy. She also kept checking their paws. During the Iditarod, dogs' paws often got cut or frozen. Race rules stated that dogs had to wear nylon boots for protection. Even so, Riddles knew their paws had to be watched carefully.

As the race went on, Riddles felt her energy level dropping. She stopped at all the necessary checkpoints; but she didn't waste any time there. She just fed her dogs, then kept going. At times she became so tired that she fell asleep while driving the dogs. She dozed off with the ropes still in her hands. Riddles' dogs were well trained. Even when she was asleep, they kept going and followed the trail.

Riddles was not the only one to sleep while driving. Other drivers, or "mushers," did the same thing. They all wanted the $50,000 prize money for winning the race.

By March 11, Riddles was in 13th place. The next day, a heavy snow began falling. The mushers had already struggled through several days of snow storms. Now they also faced dropping temperatures and high winds. By March 15, it was -40 degrees. The next day it was -53 degrees. Most mushers took long rests to recover from the terrible conditions on the trail. Riddles, however, took only short breaks. By March 16, she had passed most of the other racers.

Then Riddles entered a dangerous area filled with moose. Often these moose charged at dogs and killed them. Many mushers carried guns for protection. Riddles did not, but she kept a sharp watch for signs of trouble.

By March 17, Riddles was only 229 miles from the finish line. At the checkpoint in Shaktoolik she met the

Race Across Alaska (p. 2)

other leaders. A blizzard had forced them to stop.

"Impossible to head out into that storm," one musher said to her.

Riddles nodded. But secretly, she had other ideas. At 5:30 P.M. she slipped out of the Shaktoolik checkpoint. She and her dogs headed for Nome. The weather was terrible. Riddles and her dogs drove straight into a 40-mile-an-hour wind. Snow blew all around. At times Riddles could not even see her dogs. She got off the sled and pushed to make their load lighter. Still, after three hours, she had gone only 16 miles. Finally, she decided to stop. Her dogs curled up into tight balls to stay warm, and Riddles crawled into her sleeping bag. For 11 hours she stayed there while the storm raged all around her.

At last she decided to try again. The blizzard was still at full strength. But at least her dogs had gotten some rest. Riddles wondered if the other mushers had left Shaktoolik. She feared they might catch up to her. Nearing Norton Sound, she decided to take a shortcut. Instead of going around the bay, she would go across it.

Riddles knew she was taking a chance. Out on the ice, there were no trail markings, and there was no shelter. If the ice broke beneath the weight of Riddles' sled, she and her dogs could be killed. For hours she struggled to cross the bay. At last, she made it to the other side. She was close to the finish now, and still leading.

Finally, at 9:20 A.M. on March 20, Libby Riddles arrived in Nome. She was met by cheering crowds. Reporters were waiting to interview her. Photographers took pictures of her and her dogs. Libby Riddles had become the first woman ever to win the Iditarod.

Do You Remember?

In the blank, write the letter of the best ending for each sentence.

_____ **1.** In the Iditarod, dogs pull
    a. moose.   b. sleds.   c. logs.

_____ **2.** While driving her dogs, Riddles sometimes
    a. fell asleep.   b. sang.   c. cried.

_____ **3.** Moose often killed
    a. drivers.   b. dogs.   c. each other.

_____ **4.** Riddles took the lead by heading out into a
    a. heat wave.   b. thunderstorm.   c. blizzard.

_____ **5.** Riddles saved time by
    a. taking a shortcut.   b. changing dogs often.   c. cheating.

Race Across Alaska (p. 3)

Express Yourself

Pretend you are a newspaper reporter. You are in Nome, Alaska, when Libby Riddles arrives. On a separate piece of paper, write three or four questions you will ask Riddles.

Exploring Words

Write the correct word in each sentence.

grueling	dozed	struggled	raged	photographer
interview	recover	checkpoints	nylon	Conditions

1. To ask a person questions is to _____ that person.

2. If you fell asleep for a short time, you _____.

3. A person who takes pictures with a camera is a _____.

4. Places to stop for rest and repair along a road are called _____.

5. To get back your health or strength is to _____.

6. A strong, lightweight, man-made cloth is _____.

7. Something that is very difficult and tiring is _____.

8. If a storm hit with great force, it _____.

9. If you worked very hard to do something, you _____.

10. _____ means the way things are.

Marco Polo

Marco Polo squinted in the bright desert sun. He felt nervous. His fellow travelers told him that the bandit Nogodar often rode through this area.

"If he captures you, he will surely kill you or sell you as a slave," said a friend.

Just then another rider stopped his horse. "Look!" he shouted. He pointed to a dark cloud of dust in the distance. "It's Nogodar! He's coming this way!"

Most of the riders turned and galloped away. Marco was about to do the same. But suddenly his father, Nicolò Polo, called out to him.

"Marco! Stop! You will never outrun Nogodar. Just follow me," said Nicolò, "and you will be safe."

Silently, Marco obeyed. He knew his father was very wise. Nicolò and his brother Maffeo had spent 15 years traveling through Asia. Now, in 1271, they were making a second trip. This time they were taking 17-year-old Marco with them. Marco was delighted to be going. He wanted to share the adventures of Nicolò and Maffeo.

Nicolò told Marco to ride very slowly. "Do not kick up any dust," he warned. "It is the dust from galloping horses that Nogodar sees."

For hours the Polos crept eastward. At last they reached a valley. In it was a small city.

"Nogodar will not bother us here," said Nicolò.

Marco was happy to hear this. He later found out that Nogodar captured the men who galloped off. Some were sold as slaves. The rest were put to death.

The Polos' journey across Asia took another three years to complete. At last, in 1274, they reached China, which in those days was known as Cathay. Its leader was called a khan. In 1274, the khan was a great and powerful man named Kublai. Kublai Khan remembered Nicolò and Maffeo from their earlier trip and welcomed them warmly.

"And who is this young man?" he asked.

"Sire, it is my own son to honor you," said Nicolo.

"Welcome is he, too," said the khan.

At Kublai Khan's palace, Marco saw things which amazed him. The khan was very rich. He had huge amounts of gold, jewels, and silks. Marco had never seen so many beautiful things. Marco was also amazed by life in Cathay. The people used tools that he had never seen. They had printing presses for books. They had coal for heating water. They used paper money. Back in Europe, people had none of these things. In almost every way, Cathay was more advanced than Europe. The engineers built better bridges, the police kept better order, and the weavers made more beautiful cloth.

For the next 17 years, the Polos stayed with Kublai Khan. They became trusted friends of the khan. Marco went to different parts of Asia and brought reports back to the khan.

Marco Polo (p. 2)

Marco saw lands that no other European had ever seen. He found many strange and wonderful things. In Southern Cathay he reported seeing huge serpents. To Marco, these creatures seemed fantastic. Today they do not seem so wild. We call them crocodiles.

Although the Polos were happy in Cathay, they longed to return to Venice. One day Marco told the khan that the Polos wished to leave Cathay.

"You cannot go!" he said. "I could not bear to lose such good friends and advisers. You must never speak of it again!"

The Polos did not dare go against the orders of the khan. In 1291, however, they finally had a chance to leave. Princess Kukachin of Cathay was asked to marry the king of Persia. Men came from Persia to take the girl on the long and dangerous journey. The safest way to travel would be by sea, but the Persians did not know how to sail.

"I could go with them. I have sailed the Indian Ocean several times in my travels for you," said Marco.

The khan agreed to let Marco, Nicolò, and Maffeo sail with the princess to Persia. In return for this favor, Kublai Khan told the Polos they could return to Italy. The trip to Persia was long and difficult. It took two years to complete. From Persia, the Polos continued on to Europe. In 1295, they finally arrived in Italy.

In 1298, Marco wrote a book about his travels called *The Travels of Marco Polo*. People thought he was making up wild lies. It was only after his death that Europeans began to believe him. In the 1400s, one reader who believed him was Christopher Columbus. It was Polo's book that inspired Columbus to make his great journey.

Critical Thinking — Fact or Opinion?

A fact can be proven. An opinion is a belief. Opinions cannot be proven. Write *F* before each statement that is a fact. Write *O* before each statement that is an opinion.

_____ **1.** Marco Polo was smarter than Kublai Khan.

_____ **2.** Marco saw lands that no other European had seen.

_____ **3.** Kublai Khan was a selfish man.

_____ **4.** Marco Polo sailed across the Indian Ocean several times.

_____ **5.** Christopher Columbus believed what Marco Polo wrote.

Marco Polo (p. 3)

Do You Remember?

In the blank, write the letter of the best ending for each sentence.

_____ **1.** Nogodar was a
  a. king.   b. weaver.   c. bandit.

_____ **2.** The leader of China was called
  a. Cathay.   b. a khan.   c. Maffeo.

_____ **3.** In the 1200s, people in Europe had no
  a. horses.   b. paper money.   c. ships.

_____ **4.** Marco traveled to different parts of
  a. Asia.   b. Canada.   c. Africa.

_____ **5.** Marco helped Princess Kukachin get to
  a. Europe.   b. America.   c. Persia.

Exploring Words

Write the correct word in each sentence.

engineers	advisers	bandit
serpents	advanced	inspired

1. A person who robs and steals is a _____.

2. To be ahead of others is to be _____.

3. People who make plans for building things are _____.

4. Snakes and snake-like animals are _____.

5. If something _____ you, it made you want to do something.

6. People who help you decide what to do are _____.

Flight of the Eagle

Salomon Andrée stuck his head out the door, and a blast of cold air hit his face. Once again, the wind was blowing from the wrong direction. "Doesn't this wind ever blow from the south?" he asked himself.

Andrée, a Swedish explorer, was waiting on Danes' Island with his team. He wanted to travel in a hot-air balloon over the North Pole 720 miles away. But he needed a south wind. It never came. Finally, on August 19, 1896, he gave up. Winter was coming to the North Pole, but Andree promised, "We'll be back next year."

On May 29, 1897, Andrée and his team did return to Danes' Island. They brought with them

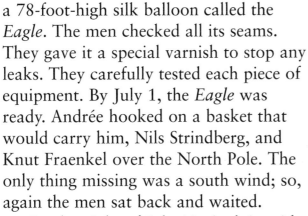

a 78-foot-high silk balloon called the *Eagle*. The men checked all its seams. They gave it a special varnish to stop any leaks. They carefully tested each piece of equipment. By July 1, the *Eagle* was ready. Andrée hooked on a basket that would carry him, Nils Strindberg, and Knut Fraenkel over the North Pole. The only thing missing was a south wind; so, again the men sat back and waited.

On the night of July 10, Andrée said, "I feel that it will not be long before we shall go up." He was right.

The next morning a joyful cry rang out. Some of the men had gotten up early. They felt the wind blowing from the

south. "Southward!" they all shouted. "A strong and steady south wind!"

Everyone jumped out of bed. Andrée met with Fraenkel, Strindberg, and the others. "Is this the day?" he asked. The wind was a bit stronger than he liked. Still, the men agreed they should go ahead. Andrée gave the order to prepare the balloon for liftoff.

Quickly the men went to work. A quiet fear gripped them all. Would the three men make it? Would they come back alive? No one had ever flown a hot-air balloon over the North Pole.

Soon the time for worrying was over, and it was time for action. Andrée jumped into the basket; Strindberg and Fraenkel followed him. At exactly 2:30 P.M., Andrée gave the order. He shouted, "Cut the ropes."

The huge balloon rose gracefully. The men on the ground cried out, "Good luck to Andrée!" The three men yelled back, "Salute old Sweden!"

At first, all went well. The balloon headed north. It rose to 1,500 feet, and traveled about 25 miles an hour. Later that day, Andrée sent back his first message by dropping a floating marker into the sea. It read, "July 11, 10 P.M. We are now over ice. Glorious weather. Excellent spirits."

On July 13, Andrée sent back another message. This time he used a carrier pigeon, and the message read simply, "Good journey northward."

The crew on the ground believed everything was going smoothly, but up in

Flight of the Eagle (p. 2)

the air, the three men must have been having trouble. After July 13, no more messages arrived. Day after day the ground crew waited, but the men were never heard from again.

Search parties were sent to look for the men. They found nothing. It seemed that their fate would be forever locked in the Arctic ice. Thirty-three years later, however, the mystery was solved. An explorer named Gunnar Horn went to White Island. There he stumbled across the frozen bodies of the three men.

Experts believe that something went wrong with the balloon, and Andrée had to make a landing. He and his men set up camp on the ice. There Strindberg died from illness or accident. Later, when Andrée and Fraenkel were cooking a meal inside their tent, a poisonous gas called carbon monoxide came from their stove. Carbon monoxide has no odor. The two men had no way of knowing that the stove was leaking. They died without knowing that they were in danger.

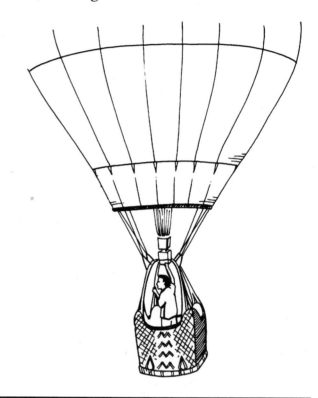

Do You Remember?

Read each sentence below. Write _T_ if the sentence is true. Write _F_ if the sentence is false.

_____ **1.** Salomon Andrée was a Swedish explorer.

_____ **2.** On Danes' Island, Andrée and his men waited for a north wind.

_____ **3.** The _Eagle_ was the name of Andrée's balloon.

_____ **4.** Andrée's balloon could travel 200 miles per hour.

_____ **5.** Andrée dropped a floating marker into the sea.

_____ **6.** Fraenkel died when he jumped out of the balloon.

_____ **7.** Gunnar Horn found the bodies of Andrée, Strindberg, and Fraenkel.

_____ **8.** Carbon monoxide has a terrible odor.

Name_____ Date_____

Flight of the Eagle (p. 3)

Critical Thinking — Main Ideas

Underline the two most important ideas from the story.

1. Salomon Andrée's balloon was a 78-foot-high silk balloon.

2. Salomon Andrée tried to reach the North Pole.

3. Gunnar Horn explored White Island in 1930.

4. Salomon Andrée never returned from his 1897 trip to the Arctic.

Exploring Words

Use the clues to complete the puzzle. Choose from the words in the box.

excellent
carrier pigeon
odor
illness
glorious
seams
fate
varnish
equipment
gracefully

Across
1. wonderful
5. bird taught to carry messages
7. being sick
9. type of paint that forms a hard, clear surface
10. what happens to a person

Down
2. smell
3. very good
4. in a smooth and easy way
6. things that have a special use
8. places where pieces of cloth are sewn together

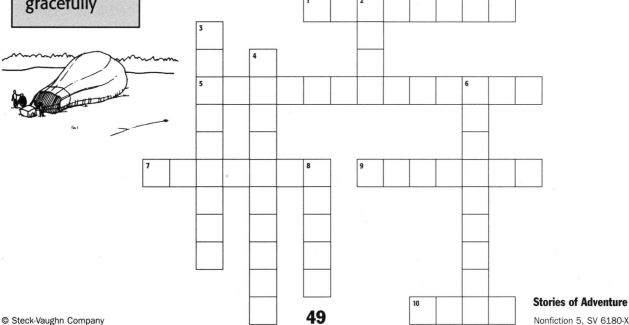

Stories of Adventure
Nonfiction 5, SV 6180-X

The Kon-Tiki

Thor Heyerdahl had made up his mind. He and five other men would sail 4,300 miles from South America to the South Sea Islands on a raft. Most sailors laughed at Heyerdahl. "Rafts are not for sailing," they told him. "They go sideways and backwards and round as the wind takes them."

Heyerdahl's friends begged him not to go. Still, Heyerdahl stuck to his plans. He wanted to test his idea that South Sea Islanders came from the South American country of Peru. Scientists laughed at this idea. They said that South America was too far away. Besides, the people of ancient Peru had no ships. Heyerdahl said the Peruvians floated across the Pacific on rafts!

In 1947, most people could not accept this idea. So Heyerdahl decided to make his own raft to sail across the ocean. He would use the same tools that the people of ancient Peru used. If he made it to the South Sea Islands, people would have to listen to him. Heyerdahl made his raft out of balsa wood logs. He named it *Kon-Tiki* after a Peruvian god. The raft was 40 feet long and 18 feet wide. There was no metal in it. After all, ancient Peruvians had no metal. Heyerdahl tied all the logs together with rope. The *Kon-Tiki* had a bamboo deck and cabin. It also had a simple square sail and a 19-foot-long steering oar.

On the morning of April 29, 1947, Heyerdahl and his crew set out. They did not know whether they would ever see land again. They had to trust the winds and the ocean currents. With luck, Heyerdahl thought, they would reach the South Sea Islands in about three months.

One expert told Heyerdahl that the logs would soak up water. A boat maker said that the ropes would never hold the wood together. Heyerdahl worried about these warnings. After all, he had never sailed a balsa wood raft before. Maybe it would sink! After a few days at sea, he saw that the logs did soak up water. When no one was looking, he poked his finger into a log. Water bubbled out. Heyerdahl then tore off a piece of the log. He dropped it into the sea and sadly watched it sink.

But the *Kon-Tiki* did not sink. Heyerdahl's crew had cut down fresh balsa trees. The sap inside the green logs sealed out the water. Only the outer inch got wet. This wet layer helped the raft. The ropes wore their way into the wet part of the wood. This protected the ropes when the logs rubbed together.

The water currents carried the *Kon-Tiki* straight toward the South Seas. On July 4, a bad storm struck. Some waves towered 25 feet above the raft. The men held tightly to the ropes as water rushed across the deck. Luckily, everyone made it, and the tough little raft proved it could weather the worst ocean storms.

A few days later, however, a sleeping bag fell over the side of the raft. Herman Watzinger reached for it, and tripped and fell into the water. Heyerdahl heard Watzinger's cry, and saw his friend

Stories of Adventure

The Kon-Tiki (p. 2)

splashing wildly in the water. "Man overboard!" he yelled.

Watzinger was a fine swimmer. But he had no chance of catching up to the raft in the rough sea. The men tossed a life belt to him, which was tied to the raft by a long rope; but the strong wind just blew the belt back. It seemed that Watzinger was lost forever. Then, suddenly, Knut Haugland grabbed the life belt and dove into the water. Haugland and Watzinger swam desperately towards each other. At last they touched hands. The four men on the raft pulled Haugland and Watzinger back to safety.

On the morning of July 30, Watzinger spotted a tiny island named Puka Puka. The raft had passed it during the night. The men tried to change course, but the current carried them away from the island. On August 3, they tried to land at another island, but the wind made it impossible.

On August 6, they spotted the dangerous Raroia coral reef. Waves crashed angrily against the sharp rocks.

They didn't want to land here! But they had no choice. As the *Kon-Tiki* drifted toward shore, the men got ready for the worst.

Heyerdahl made one final note in his book. "Very close now. Drifting along the reef. Only a hundred yards or so away. Must pack up the log now. All in good spirits; it looks bad, but we shall make it!"

As the *Kon-Tiki* drifted closer, one huge wave after another battered the men and the raft. Then the biggest wave of all smashed the raft like a toy against the reef. The *Kon-Tiki* was now nothing but a tangle of twisted logs. Yet somehow the men managed to hang onto it. Finally the raft reached the rocks. The men climbed off the raft and made their way to the shore.

Thor Heyerdahl had made it. He had proven that it was possible to float across the Pacific on a raft. His trip forced scientists to think differently, and people saw that Thor Heyerdahl wasn't crazy after all.

Do You Remember?

In the blank, write the letter of the best ending for each sentence.

_____ **1.** Heyerdahl believed that the first South Sea Islanders came from
   a. Europe.   b. South America.   c. Africa.

_____ **2.** Heyerdahl and his crew made their raft out of
   a. balsa wood.   b. coral.   c. metal.

_____ **3.** *Kon-Tiki* was the name of
   a. Heyerdahl's wife.   b. a Peruvian god.   c. an island.

_____ **4.** A boat maker told Heyerdahl that his raft would
   a. be hit by lightning.   b. be eaten by sharks.   c. fall apart.

_____ **5.** Herman Watzinger almost died when
   a. he fell overboard.   b. Haugland hit him.   c. he became ill.

The Kon-Tiki (p. 3)

Express Yourself

Pretend you are Thor Heyerdahl's son or daughter. Your father is getting ready to sail the *Kon-Tiki* across the Pacific. What would you want to say to him before he left? Write your thoughts on a separate piece of paper.

Exploring Words

Use the clues to complete the puzzle. Choose from the words in the box.

backwards
coral reef
ancient
balsa
currents
sap
warnings
desperately

Across
2. very old
6. being told about danger
7. wildly
8. the juice inside plants

Down
1. with the back part in front
3. a thin wall of stony material
4. a strong, light kind of wood
5. water that moves a certain direction

The Secrets of Stonehenge

Darkness hangs over Salisbury, England. The meadows near the town are wrapped in silence and fog. Then the sun begins to rise. The fog lifts, and something amazing comes into view. It is a ring of huge gray stones. Each stone is 7 feet wide and 13 feet tall, and has been standing in this location for over 3,500 years. Together, these stones form an old ruin called Stonehenge.

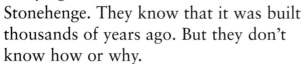

Scientists have spent many years studying Stonehenge. They know that it was built thousands of years ago. But they don't know how or why.

The stones that form the circle each weighs from 30 to 50 tons. At one time there were 30 of these giant stones. Today only 17 remain standing.

The standing stones supported other stones that were placed on top of them. Inside the large circle was a smaller circle made of bluestones. Inside of it stood two sets of stones forming horseshoes.

All of the stones have been carefully carved. They have round edges and curved sides. Scientists are not sure how the builders shaped the stones. These early people had few tools, yet somehow, they chipped away at the huge stones. They carved knobs on the tops of some, and dug holes into others. The knobs and holes fit each other perfectly and hold the stones on top. Carpenters still use the same method today.

The stones of Stonehenge did not come from the fields around Salisbury. Is it possible that the builders transported the stones from some distant spot? Scientists think that this is what they must have done. The largest stones are made of sandstone. They may have come from a sandstone pit about 20 miles away. The smaller ones were probably carried even farther. The four-ton stones in the inner circle are made of bluestone. The nearest source of bluestone is the Prescelly Mountains in Wales. That is more than 200 miles away from Stonehenge!

How did the builders get the stones to Salisbury? They had no machines. They had no horses or carts. Yet somehow, they moved the huge stones. Scientists think they used some kind of wooden sled. The stones could have been tied to the sled with ropes. It would have taken hundreds of workers to move the stones. Some would have pulled the sled while others pushed it. Other people think the stones were put on rafts and floated along the coast and down the rivers.

Once the stones reached Salisbury, the builders had to raise the biggest stones so that they would stand up. Then they had to lay the other stones across the top. It sounds impossible, but somehow, the builders found a way.

Stonehenge is full of puzzles. One puzzle is a ring of 56 holes around the outside of the stones. A man named John Aubrey discovered the holes 300 years ago. Today they are called the Aubrey

The Secrets of Stonehenge (p. 2)

holes. The people who built Stonehenge dug these holes and then filled them in. Each hole is about two feet deep and three feet wide. They are all the same distance apart. What were these holes used for? Some scientists think they were used to bury the dead. Scientists have found human bones in the holes. They have also found animal bones and bits of pottery, but no one knows for certain why the holes were dug.

Why did early people build Stonehenge? Over the years, scientists have had many ideas. Some think Stonehenge was some sort of temple. Maybe people worshipped the sun or sky here. Maybe it was a place for practicing magic. Or perhaps it was used for large group meetings.

In 1963, a scientist named Gerald Hawkins came up with another idea. He numbered each stone and each Aubrey hole. He measured the exact angle from each stone to the sun. Hawkins fed all his numbers into a computer. Hawkins found out that the stones and holes often lined up with the sun. They showed the first day of each season. June 21, for example, is the first day of summer. On that day, the rising sun lines up with one stone arch. Hawkins decided Stonehenge was used as a giant calendar. He believed early people used it to study the movement of the sun, moon, and stars.

Not all scientists think Hawkins is right. The people who built Stonehenge had no written language. They did not leave an explanation of why they built Stonehenge. Scientists continue to look for new evidence to unlock the secret.

In the meantime, the mystery of Stonehenge remains. The stones may never give us the answers we want. But they will always be symbols of a forgotten past.

Do You Remember?

In the blank, write the letter of the best ending for each sentence.

_____ **1.** The stones in Stonehenge form a large
    a. triangle.   b. square.   c. circle.

_____ **2.** The stones might have been brought to Salisbury by
    a. truck.   b. raft.   c. horses.

_____ **3.** The builders of Stonehenge did not have
    a. a written language.   b. food.   c. friends.

_____ **4.** The Aubrey holes contain bits of
    a. clothing.   b. pottery.   c. diamonds.

_____ **5.** Gerald Hawkins thought Stonehenge was a giant
    a. dance hall.   b. calendar.   c. fake.

The Secrets of Stonehenge (p. 3)

Critical Thinking — Fact or Opinion?

A fact can be proven. An opinion is a belief. Opinions cannot be proven. Write **F** before each statement that is a fact. Write **O** before each statement that is an opinion.

_____ **1.** Stonehenge can be found near Salisbury, England.

_____ **2.** Scientists should take Stonehenge apart and study the stones more carefully.

_____ **3.** There are 56 holes known as Aubrey holes.

_____ **4.** Gerald Hawkins was the smartest man who ever lived.

_____ **5.** Some of the stones at Stonehenge weigh 50 tons.

Exploring Words

Read each sentence. Fill in the circle next to the best meaning for the word in dark print. If you need help, use a dictionary.

1. The builders chose a **location** near Salisbury, England.
  ⓐ place   ⓑ distance   ⓒ color

2. The stones were **transported** from far away.
  ⓐ welcomed   ⓑ burned   ⓒ dragged

3. Some people think Stonehenge was a **place of worship**.
  ⓐ temple   ⓑ store   ⓒ hiding place

4. Hawkins checked the **angle** of the stones to the sun.
  ⓐ time   ⓑ footprints   ⓒ measurement of slant

5. The Aubrey holes contain certain **evidence**.
  ⓐ drawings   ⓑ guiding information   ⓒ animals

6. No one knows the **precise** purpose of the Aubrey holes.
  ⓐ exact   ⓑ long ago   ⓒ secret

Nonfiction 5, SV 6180-X

Designs in the Desert

Can you imagine a spider that is 150 feet long? Have you ever seen a lizard that is nearly 600 feet long? Did you know there was a bird that measures more than 900 feet tall?

Such creatures can be found in the desert of Peru, a country in South America. They don't spin webs, crawl, or fly. The spider, lizard, and bird are three of the more than 100 drawings made by Nazca Indians about 2,000 years ago.

The Nazca lines cover an area of about 200 square miles (518 square kilometers). Each line was made by scraping away stones to show the yellow soil beneath. Most of the lines are only a few inches wide. Stones are piled along both sides of the lines. It is believed that all the work was done by hand.

The Nazca lines are hard to see if a person is standing on the ground. Most of the drawings are so enormous that the shapes can only be recognized from high above the ground. Why did the Nazca people make the drawings so large?

There are countless lines. Some are more than five miles long, and one is almost 40 miles long. Some stretch over mountains, form squares or triangles, or the shapes of animals, plants, and people.

The Nazca Indians lived in the desert, but they drew many animals that do not live in the desert. They drew a picture of a whale. They also drew a spider that lives only in the jungle. The drawing of the spider is perfect in all details. It even shows a part of the spider that can only be seen with a microscope. Yet the huge drawing was made before the microscope was invented.

How did the Nazca Indians plan the drawings? Most of the pictures can only be recognized from high above the ground. In order to see a complete drawing, one has to be at least 1,000 feet above the ground. How did they check to make sure the details of the drawings were correct?

It is possible that the Nazca Indians climbed to nearby hilltops to check their work, but some people believe the Indians flew in hot-air balloons to look at the drawings. Scientists got this idea from the Nazca pottery. Some of the paintings on the pottery show balloons or kites flying high in the sky.

The Nazca Indians made a very light, fine cloth. This material has been found in Nazcan tombs. It could have been used to make the hot-air balloons. Air would not have leaked through this material. There are large circles of blackened rocks at the end of many of the Nazca lines. Some people believe that fires were built there to heat the air for the balloons.

Other people believe that visitors from outer space helped make the lines. They

Designs in the Desert (p. 2)

say some of these lines might have been made by spaceships taking off or landing in the desert.

The Nazca Indians had no written language. They left no record to explain the lines. Maybe the Nazca Indians saw the shapes of animals in the stars, and then they drew these shapes in the desert.

Some people believe the Nazca lines form a calendar. This calendar was used to tell the positions of the sun, moon, planets, and stars. By using the calendar, the Nazca Indians could tell when to plant crops. They could tell when the seasons would change. Maybe it helped them know when to gather their crops.

Scientists have studied these lines for more than 60 years, but no clear answers have been found. These desert designs from long ago remain a mystery.

Do You Remember?

Read each sentence below. Write *T* if the sentence is true. Write *F* if the sentence is false.

_____ **1.** The Nazca Indian drawings are very small.

_____ **2.** The Nazca Indians lived 2,000 years ago.

_____ **3.** One Nazca drawing shows a jungle spider.

_____ **4.** The Nazca Indians made a very fine cloth.

_____ **5.** Most of the drawings can only be seen from 1,000 feet above the ground.

_____ **6.** Scientists have found the hot-air balloons used by Nazca Indians.

_____ **7.** The Nazca people did not make pottery.

_____ **8.** Nazca Indians wrote many books explaining their drawings.

Designs in the Desert (p. 3)

Express Yourself

You are flying in an airplane over Peru. You look out the window and see the Nazca lines. On a separate piece of paper, write a letter home telling what you saw and how it made you feel.

Exploring Words 🔍

Use the clues to complete the puzzle. Choose from the words in the box.

| triangles |
| lizard |
| enormous |
| scraping |
| tombs |
| soil |
| details |
| countless |
| positions |
| material |

Across
3. too many to be counted
5. cloth
8. small parts of a larger thing
9. place where people are buried
10. dirt

Down
1. rubbing with a sharp instrument
2. huge
4. shapes with three sides
6. a reptile
7. places where things are

Stories of Mystery

An Island of Giants

The young boy ran to the rock quarry. He had to warn the sculptors who were working there.

"Quick!" he shouted when he reached them. "Come quickly! War has broken out on the island!"

The sculptors dropped their tools and ran to get their weapons. One sculptor stopped and took a final look around the quarry. He didn't want to leave. He wanted to finish carving the giant stone statues they called moai (MOH eye).

The people of Easter Island were skilled sculptors. Their life on the island was good. They had much to eat. They built and lived in fine houses, and the islanders were very proud of the moai.

It was about 1600 when war broke out on Easter Island. No one knows how long the war lasted, but when the fighting stopped, the island had changed forever. The war destroyed almost everything. Many people had died. Some people did survive, but they had to start a new life from the ruins. The rich culture of the earlier days disappeared. They had no time for carving the moai; they spent their days working hard for the food and water they needed in order to stay alive.

For years the moai were forgotten. Then, in the 1700s, Dutch sailors discovered Easter Island. They were stunned by the moai. The sailors stared at the 12-foot and 30-foot statues lining the beach. As time went by, other people found the island, and they too were impressed by the statues.

In the 1880s, scientists took a closer look at Easter Island and the moai. By then there were only a few islanders left. These islanders knew very little about the moai.

The scientists were amazed by what they found. There were over 700 statues on the island. Some were standing on stone bases, but others had been knocked over. Still other statues lay unfinished in the quarry.

The moai were carved in the same style. All stood with their backs to the ocean, and all had huge heads and the same unsmiling face. The statues had no legs. They had long ears and arms that hung stiffly at their sides. Some of the moai wore huge hats made of red stone.

Perhaps one day the secrets of the moai may be known. Until then many questions remain. What happened to the sculptors of these silent figures? How were the moai placed on the stone bases? Why were they so big? What purpose did they serve?

Scientists found that some of the moai are very old. The oldest ones have been around for over 1,000 years. They were built with stone picks and axes. All the statues are very heavy. Most weigh about 20 tons. The biggest one weighs 90 tons.

An Island of Giants (p. 2)

Scientists know that the sculptors carved the statues from soft rock. The rock came from a quarry on one corner of the island. Some of the carving tools

were found scattered about the quarry.

Scientists believe the statues were carved to honor the dead, but they don't know why so many were built. Nor do they know why they are all alike.

The early islanders must have had a

large and strong community. It would have taken many people to build and move all the moai. But then something happened. For some reason, war broke out, and the community fell apart. This explains why some statues were never finished, and why some were knocked over. It also explains why sculptors dropped their tools so suddenly.

The full story of Easter Island will never be known. There was a time when the island was a happy, lively place. People worked together and shared a common purpose. But that time is gone forever. All that remain are the moai. They stand tall and silent — never smiling, never blinking, and never telling the secrets of the past.

Do You Remember?

Read each sentence below. Write *T* if the sentence is true. Write *F* if the sentence is false.

_____ **1.** The statues face the ocean.

_____ **2.** The statues on Easter Island have smiling faces.

_____ **3.** The statues have long ears and large heads.

_____ **4.** The builders carved the statues from tree trunks.

_____ **5.** The biggest statue weighs 90 tons.

_____ **6.** The statues were all carved by the same person.

_____ **7.** There are hundreds of statues on Easter Island.

_____ **8.** No one knows why the builders made the statues so big.

An Island of Giants (p. 3)

Critical Thinking — Main Ideas

Underline the two most important ideas from the story.

1. Easter Island is covered with 700 huge statues.

2. The builders of the statues had much to eat.

3. We will never know why the moai were built.

4. Some statues wore huge hats made of red stone.

Exploring Words

Choose the correct word from the box to complete each sentence.

quarry	sculptors	stunned
culture	moai	survive

1. A pit where rocks are cut or dug out is a _____.

2. If you see something you don't believe, you are _____.

3. To live through something dangerous is to_____.

4. People who carve statues are _____.

5. The giant stone statues carved on Easter Island are

known as _____.

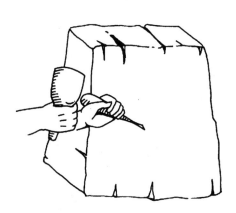

6. The way people live during a certain time is

called their _____.

Triangle of Fear

The *Vagabond,* a 20-foot boat, rocked silently in the waves. On July 6, 1969, a Swedish crew found the *Vagabond* in the waters of the Bermuda Triangle. Several crew members boarded the boat and found the logbook. It had last been written in on July 2. Everything on board was in place, but there was no sign of the *Vagabond's* crew. Nothing was ever found to explain what caused the *Vagabond* to be abandoned or what became of its crew. Many blame the Triangle for this unsolved disappearance.

The Bermuda Triangle covers hundreds of miles of the Atlantic Ocean.  Its boundaries are formed by lines that run from the island of Bermuda, to Florida, and to the West Indies. Most ships and planes cross the Triangle safely, but over 1,000 people have disappeared in the Triangle. No one knows how or why it happens.

One of the most famous ships lost in the Bermuda Triangle was the *Cyclops,* a huge Navy coal ship. On March 13, 1918, there were 309 people on board. The weather was clear. The ship's radio was in working order. But somewhere inside the Bermuda Triangle, the ship and its crew disappeared. The giant *Cyclops* was never seen or heard from again. It never radioed for help.

The Navy was surprised to learn the *Cyclops* was missing. They searched for wreckage for over a month but found

nothing. The *Cyclops* and its passengers had vanished without a trace.

On December 5, 1945, a group of five Navy planes took off from Florida. The pilots were on a regular training flight called Flight 19. As the pilots flew into the Bermuda Triangle, everything seemed normal. For hours they flew without problems. Several times they reported their position to the control tower. But at 3:15 P.M., the flight leader sent out a strange message.

"Calling tower. This is an emergency. We seem to be off course. We cannot see land. Repeat. We cannot see land. We are not sure of our position. We seem to be lost. Everything is wrong. Even the ocean doesn't look as it should." The flight leader reported that they seemed to be 200 miles northeast of Miami, Florida. That was the last message received by the tower from Flight 19.

The Navy quickly sent out a large seaplane to find the planes and rescue the pilots. One of the officers on the seaplane reported strong winds in the area where the missing planes had been. That was the last message received from the seaplane. Then it and its crew of 13 disappeared as well.

The Navy sent out 250 planes, boats, and seaplanes to search the area. The search lasted for five days, but the searchers found no bodies, no sign of wreckage, and no oil spills on the water. Yet, 27 men and 6 planes had mysteriously vanished!

Many people who have traveled in the

Triangle of Fear (p. 2)

Bermuda Triangle have reported some kind of trouble, but they have escaped without harm. Two of the lucky ones were Betty and Warren Miller. In June 1975, they were flying their small plane through the Triangle. Suddenly, they were surrounded by yellow fog. They couldn't see a thing. Warren Miller tried to check his position, but all the instruments in the plane had stopped working. The radio, too, was dead.

For two frightening hours, the Millers didn't know where they were or which way they were going. The yellow fog stayed with them wherever they went.

Finally, the fog lifted. All at once, the plane's instruments began working again. The Millers followed a radio signal to Florida. They landed quickly. They then asked mechanics at the airport to check their plane. Mechanics found nothing wrong with any part of the plane. The Millers checked the weather reports for that day. No one else had seen any kind of yellow fog.

Others tell the same kinds of stories. Some people have felt their ships pulled by an unseen force. Some have even seen strange bright lights. Their planes' instruments have stopped working. All of these people have lost radio contact with the outside world. All have felt in danger of being lost forever.

The unexplained disappearances continue, and there will probably be more reports from those who escape the Triangle. But no one really knows what goes on in this eerie part of the Atlantic Ocean.

Do You Remember?

Read each sentence below. Write _T_ if the sentence is true. Write _F_ if the sentence is false.

_____ **1.** The Bermuda Triangle lies in the Indian Ocean.

_____ **2.** Over 1,000 people have disappeared in the Bermuda Triangle.

_____ **3.** The planes from Flight 19 were never found.

_____ **4.** Betty and Warren Miller were killed in the Bermuda Triangle.

_____ **5.** Mechanics found nothing wrong with the Millers' plane.

Triangle of Fear (p. 3)

Critical Thinking — Drawing Conclusions

Finish each sentence by writing the best answer.

1. The Swedish crew who found the *Vagabond* was puzzled because _____

   _____.

2. The disappearance of the *Cyclops* was strange because _____

   _____.

3. Betty and Warren Miller were frightened by the yellow fog because _____

   _____.

4. The Millers asked mechanics to check their plane because _____

   _____.

Exploring Words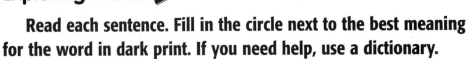

Read each sentence. Fill in the circle next to the best meaning for the word in dark print. If you need help, use a dictionary.

1. The **boundaries** of the Triangle are formed by lines that run from Bermuda, to Florida, and to the West Indies.

   ⓐ states   ⓑ edges   ⓒ boxes

2. For some reason, the sailors had **abandoned** the ship.

   ⓐ burned down   ⓑ become afraid of   ⓒ left

3. Everything seemed **normal**.

   ⓐ ordinary   ⓑ small   ⓒ twisted

4. **Mechanics** found nothing wrong with the plane.

   ⓐ people who work on machines   ⓑ sailors   ⓒ reporters

5. The Millers thought the yellow fog was **eerie**.

   ⓐ dirty   ⓑ strange and scary   ⓒ pretty

6. The Millers were not in **contact** with the radio tower.

   ⓐ in need of   ⓑ in touch with   ⓒ in a hurry

Stories of Mystery

What Happened to Amelia?

The crew of the *Itasca* waited eagerly for a message from Amelia Earhart. At 2:45 A.M., they heard her voice.

"Cloudy weather, cloudy," she said.

Her voice could hardly be heard above the crackle of the radio, but the crew was excited. Soon she should be passing over the ship. She was trying to set a new flying record, and the crew on the *Itasca* was proud to help her do it.

It was July 2, 1937. Earhart was more than halfway through a flight around 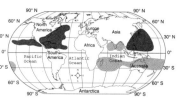 the world. No one had ever made such a trip. By July 1, she had completed 22,000 miles. That left only 7,000 miles to go. The most dangerous part of the trip remained. She would take off from New Guinea and fly 2,500 miles. She would have to find and land on tiny Howland Island in the middle of miles and miles of ocean. She would have no landmarks to follow. She had Fred Noonan, a navigator, with her; but even so, the journey would be dangerous.

The Coast Guard ship *Itasca* was anchored near Howland Island. They would give her directions by radio.

After many hours, Earhart sent her first message to the *Itasca*. Over the next six hours, the crew received several messages from her. But she never talked long enough for radio operator Leo Bellarts to figure out where she was. Earhart kept switching her radio to different channels.

By 7:30 A.M., the crew was worried. Earhart was running late. At 7:42 A.M., she sent another message.

"We must be on you but cannot see you. Gas is running low. Have been unable to reach you by radio. We are flying at 1,000 feet."

Bellarts tried frantically to reach Earhart. He had no success.

At 7:58 A.M., her voice came in again. "We are circling but cannot see the island. Cannot hear you."

She sounded tense now, almost scared, and the crew feared the worst. At 8:44 A.M., they heard, "We are on the line of position 157-337. We are running north and south."

Those were the last words anyone ever heard from Amelia Earhart.

The United States Navy sent out a huge search party for the missing plane. The searchers found no sign of it. Meanwhile, people everywhere were asking the same question. What went wrong?

The Navy said Earhart must have run out of gas. Her plane crashed in the ocean. She and Noonan died at sea.

Not everyone accepted this story. Rumors began to spread. One rumor was that Earhart couldn't find Howland Island, so she landed on one of the Marshall Islands. She and Noonan became prisoners of the Japanese.

Another rumor was that Earhart had not flown straight for Howland, but had been on a spy mission for the United States. Earhart was trying to see if Japan

What Happened to Amelia? (p. 2)

was building army bases on the Marshall Islands. If this rumor is true, members of the search party had been looking in the wrong spot. In the 1960s, several people went to the Marshalls. They talked to many natives.

Some of these natives remembered seeing a plane crash in 1937. These natives said two Americans, a man and a woman, were in the plane. The natives had never seen a woman pilot.

This was exciting information. It suggested Earhart and Noonan *had* gone down in the Marshalls, and that they lived through the crash. The natives said they were taken prisoner by the Japanese. The Japanese didn't want anyone to know about their army bases, so they kept the pair locked up. Finally, both got sick and died.

Year after year, Americans searched the Marshalls. In 1968, they found pieces of an old American plane. Searchers also found a grave with a few human bones. Were these the bones of Earhart and Noonan?

One writer believes that Earhart was held prisoner by the Japanese until the end of World War II. She made it back to the United States but wanted to escape reporters, so she moved to New Jersey and took the name Irene Bolam. But the woman named Bolam said she was not Earhart.

The whole story may never be known. The last flight of Amelia Earhart may always remain one of the world's great mysteries.

Do You Remember?

Read each sentence below. Write *T* if the sentence is true. Write *F* if the sentence is false.

_____ **1.** The radio operator from the *Itasca* had long conversations with Earhart.

_____ **2.** Fred Noonan was Earhart's navigator.

_____ **3.** Amelia Earhart never reached Howland Island.

_____ **4.** Irene Bolam claimed to be Amelia Earhart.

_____ **5.** Searchers found a photograph showing Earhart in a Japanese prison.

Name _____ Date _____

What Happened to Amelia? (p. 3)

Express Yourself

Imagine you are a reporter writing about the disappearance of Amelia Earhart. Tell who, what, when, where, and why in your newspaper article. Use a separate piece of paper.

Exploring Words

Use the clues to complete the puzzle. Choose from the words in the box.

| landmarks |
| navigator |
| anchored |
| frantically |
| rumors |
| mission |
| base |
| natives |
| grave |

Across

5. people born in a certain place
8. statements that have not been proven true
9. person who plans the travel path of an airplane

Down

1. things that can help a person find the way
2. a place run by the army or other military forces
3. in an excited, worried way
4. a special job to be done
6. a hole in the ground for burying a dead body
7. held in place

A Spaceship Adventure

The night was dark and silent as Betty and Barney Hill drove down a deserted New Hampshire road. Betty had been watching a bright light in the sky. Barney thought it might be a satellite. As the Hills drove on, they became frightened. The bright light was coming from a large, flat object, and this object was following them!

Barney drove to the side of the road and stopped. He got out of the car and walked across a field to get a closer look at the object. He found himself moving toward it. It was now about 50 feet away from him. Barney looked through his binoculars. He saw about six strange-looking creatures looking down at him from inside the object. They had big heads and shiny eyes.

Barney was frightened, but he couldn't stop looking or run away. Betty was screaming at him from the car. Using all his strength, he pulled the glasses from his eyes and ran back to the car and sped away. The object mysteriously disappeared.

As they came to the town of Ashland, they suddenly heard a strange beeping sound. They felt themselves getting very sleepy. Then their minds went blank. Some time later, Betty and Barney remember hearing the beeping again. They looked at a road sign. They were now 35 miles south of Ashland. Neither one could remember driving the 35 miles. Their watches, they noticed, had stopped.

When they got home, they saw it had taken them two hours longer than usual to make the trip.

Both Betty and Barney were upset. They tried to forget the whole thing, but they began having terrible nightmares. At last they went to see Dr. Benjamin Simon. Dr. Simon hypnotized people to help them remember things.

Dr. Simon hypnotized Barney first. For the first time, Barney could remember what had happened to him.

He said, "I drove quite a few miles. Then I saw a group of men standing in the highway. They came towards me. I felt very weak, but I wasn't afraid. They took me into their spaceship.

"I was taken to a hospital operating room. It was pale blue—sky blue. And I closed my eyes. I was lying on a table, and I thought someone was putting a cup on the top of my leg. And then it stopped. I got off the table and was guided back to my car. Then I saw Betty coming down the road, and she got into the car, too.

"Then the flying object was going. It was a bright, huge ball—orange. It was a beautiful bright ball. Then it was gone. Betty and I were left in darkness. We began driving. And then we heard the beeping."

Dr. Simon listened to Barney's story. He wasn't sure what to think. Dr. Simon couldn't quite believe that Barney had been taken aboard a spaceship. He thought Barney might have dreamed the whole thing. He decided to hypnotize

A Spaceship Adventure (p. 2)

Betty. Betty did not know what Barney had said to Dr. Simon. But under hypnosis, she told the same story. She saw men standing in the road. They came up to the car and took her and Barney aboard their spaceship. Betty said they put her on a hospital room table.

"They pushed up the sleeve of my dress, and they looked at my arm. They scraped my arms to get little pieces of skin."

Betty said the leader then showed her a book, which contained a map of the stars. It showed where the spaceship had been and where it was going. Then the space creatures led her back to the car.

When Betty finished her story, Dr. Simon was even more confused. Neither Betty nor Barney knew what the other had told Dr. Simon. But they had ended up with the same story. Was it possible that they really *had* been taken aboard a spacecraft?

Other questions remained. Betty had never studied the stars, but she was able to draw a map like the one she had seen in the spaceship. Her map showed the correct position of dozens of stars.

Barney developed a strange ring of warts on his leg. These warts formed a perfect circle. They were in the same spot where Barney said the cup had been placed.

How could all of this be explained? Dr. Simon wasn't sure. Other experts studied the case. No one really knows what happened to Betty and Barney Hill. Perhaps they had the same dream. Or perhaps Betty had the dream, and Barney somehow read her mind. Or maybe, just maybe, their story is true.

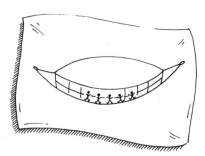

Do You Remember?

In the blank, write the letter of the best ending for each sentence.

_____ **1.** The space creatures had
   a. no eyes.   b. shiny eyes.   c. four eyes.

_____ **2.** Betty said the space creatures took little pieces of her
   a. skin.   b. hair.   c. nails.

_____ **3.** The Hills went to Dr. Simon to get
   a. help.   b. weapons.   c. money.

_____ **4.** Barney developed a strange
   a. cough.   b. ring of warts.   c. laugh.

_____ **5.** Betty said the leader of the space creatures showed her a
   a. flower.   b. movie.   c. map.

A Spaceship Adventure (p. 3)

Critical Thinking — Finding the Sequence ⚡

Number the sentences to show the order in which things happened in the story.

_____ The Hills heard a beeping sound.

_____ Dr. Simon hypnotized Barney.

_____ Barney thought he saw a satellite.

_____ The Hills began having nightmares.

_____ Betty drew a map of the stars.

Exploring Words 🔍

Read each sentence. Fill in the circle next to the best meaning for the word in dark print. If you need help, use a dictionary.

1. Barney developed **warts** on his leg.
   ⓐ small, hard bumps on the skin   ⓑ hair   ⓒ stripes
2. Barney thought the light came from a **satellite**.
   ⓐ street light
   ⓑ forest fire
   ⓒ object that circles Earth or the moon
3. Betty and Barney's minds were **blank**.
   ⓐ in severe pain
   ⓑ moving quickly
   ⓒ empty
4. Barney had a pair of **binoculars**.
   ⓐ old pants
   ⓑ two telescopes that have been joined together
   ⓒ slippers
5. Dr. Simon decided to **hypnotize** the Hills.
   ⓐ photograph   ⓑ test   ⓒ put into a deep sleep
6. Betty and Barney had **nightmares**.
   ⓐ phone calls   ⓑ frightening dreams   ⓒ big dinners

Stories of Mystery

Balloon Ride to Freedom

"We have to escape," said Peter Strelzyk.

"Yes, but how?" asked Gunter Wetzel.

"We can't walk across the border. The guards will shoot us. And we can't swim across. There are bombs all along the banks of the river."

Peter whispered, "We could cross the border in a hot-air balloon."

"And where do we find a hot-air balloon?" laughed Gunter.

"We don't find one. We make our own," replied Peter.

Peter Strelzyk and Gunter Wetzel lived in East Germany. The Communists controlled East Germany, and they didn't allow people much freedom. The two men decided that to find freedom, they would have to take their families to West Germany.

On March 7, 1978, Peter came up with the idea of the balloon. The two men knew nothing about balloons, and they couldn't find any books on the subject. They decided to try it anyway. They bought 880 yards of brown cotton in a nearby town. They told the salesperson they were making tents for young people at a camp.

They took the material to Gunter's house. Secretly, they worked on the balloon in the attic. Gunter and his wife, Petra, sewed the cotton into the shape of a balloon. Peter built a little platform for it.

After six weeks, the balloon was ready to test. They tried to inflate the balloon, but nothing happened. The air just leaked through the material. Sadly, they took the balloon home, cut it into small pieces, and burned it.

For several months, Peter and Gunter looked for a better type of cloth. They decided on taffeta. They drove to a different town to buy the 880 yards of material. This time they told the salesperson they belonged to a sailing club.

As the second balloon took shape, Gunter started to have second thoughts and decided not to try to escape.

Peter Strelzyk continued to work on the balloon alone. In June 1979, the balloon was finished. Peter and his family waited for the right weather. On the night of July 3, the wind began blowing toward the West German border.

They and their two children drove to a quiet spot near the border, and Peter inflated the balloon. It took him just five minutes. The four of them jumped onto the tiny platform. The balloon rose slowly into the sky. For 34 minutes, it stayed up. Then a thick fog moved into the area, and the balloon became wet. The extra weight dragged it back to the ground. They landed in the woods.

Peter looked around in panic. Were they in East Germany or West Germany? He saw the high wire fences that marked the border. With a sinking heart, he knew he and his family were still in East Germany. They got home before the police saw them, but they had to leave their balloon stuck in the treetops.

Balloon Ride to Freedom (p. 2)

Within a few days, the police found the wrecked balloon. They vowed to find the owners of the balloon and put them in jail.

Peter was afraid. He had to build a new balloon fast. Later that month, he asked Gunter to join him again. Gunter agreed.

This time, they didn't dare buy the 880 yards of cloth they needed from one store. That would make the police suspicious. So, each day they drove to different towns. They bought a few yards here and a few yards there. In all, they drove more than 2,400 miles and went to nearly 100 towns. The two families used all the money they had in savings.

For weeks they worked around-the-clock sewing the pieces together. When they finished, it was one of the largest hot-air balloons ever made in Europe.

On September 15, the two families drove out of town. On an empty field, they filled the balloon, and all eight people hopped on board.

Soon they were 6,500 feet above the ground. Then suddenly, they saw searchlights. Peter turned up the flame, and the balloon rose to 8,500 feet. The searchlight couldn't shine that high, but at this height, it was freezing cold. The children huddled together trying not to cry.

For 23 minutes, they stayed high in the air, but then they ran out of gas, and the balloon began to fall. Five minutes later, it hit the ground with a thud.

They did not know if they were safe. Leaving their wives and children hidden, the two men walked toward a barn. A police car approached them.

"Are we in West Germany?" Peter asked.

"Yes," answered one of the police officers.

Peter and Gunter hugged each other in joy. "We've done it! We've done it!" they cried. And so they had. They were the first people ever to fly a balloon to freedom.

Do You Remember?

In the blank, write the letter of the best ending for each sentence.

_____ **1.** Peter Strelzyk and Gunter Wetzel wanted to get to
   a. East Germany.   b. West Germany.   c. Poland.

_____ **2.** The balloon made of cotton cloth
   a. burned up.   b. leaked air.   c. was too heavy.

_____ **3.** Peter Strelzyk and his family left the second balloon in the
   a. treetops.   b. ocean.   c. back of a police car.

_____ **4.** The third balloon carried
   a. Peter and his wife.   b. Gunter.   c. both families.

Stories of Escape

Nonfiction 5, SV 6180-X

Balloon Ride to Freedom (p. 3)

Express Yourself

Pretend you are the son or daughter of Peter Strelzyk. You and your family have escaped by balloon to West Germany. On a separate piece of paper, write a letter to a friend in East Germany describing your escape.

Exploring Words

Use the words in the box to complete the paragraphs. Reread the paragraphs to be sure they make sense.

Communists	clues	taffeta	vowed	height	inflate

Peter Strelzyk and Gunter Wetzel did not like living in East Germany because it

was controlled by **(1)** _____.

Finally, they decided to escape in a hot-air balloon.

Their first balloon leaked when they tried to

(2) _____ it. They made a second balloon of

(3) _____. This balloon fell to the ground and was later found by police

who **(4)** _____ they would put the owners in jail.

The third balloon took the Strelzyk and Wetzel families to a **(5)** _____

of 8,500 feet. When they landed, they searched for **(6)** _____ to find

out where they were. They were happy when they learned they had made it to

West Germany.

Lawyer Turns Outlaw

Tim Kirk sat in a small room in Brushy Mountain State Prison in Knoxville, Tennessee. Across from him sat his lawyer, Mary Evans. She would be defending the 36-year-old prisoner against the new charges brought against him.

Kirk's trial was to start soon. He was already serving a 65-year sentence for armed robbery. Now he was accused of killing two prisoners and wounding two other prisoners. This time he could be put to death.

It didn't look good, but Kirk wasn't worried. He didn't plan to be around for the trial.

Mary Evans met Tim Kirk in August 1982, when she was given his case. She was a bright, successful, 27-year-old lawyer, but something happened while she was trying to defend Kirk that would change her life forever.

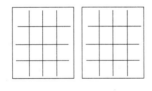

Since their first meeting, Evans had made 21 trips to the prison to prepare for Kirk's murder trial. They had been alone in the visitors' room only twice. The prison guards never noticed anything unusual about the visits.

But somehow Kirk had talked Evans into helping him escape. A week before the trial, they made their plans. Kirk asked Evans to bring some heavy tape and street clothes with her on the day of the escape. He also asked her to bring two guns.

Soon after her last meeting with Kirk, Evans went to prison officials. She said, "I want a doctor to give Tim Kirk some tests. I need the results for his trial."

Officials set up the tests with Dr. Gary Salk. On March 31, 1983, three guards took Kirk to Dr. Salk's office. Mary Evans was waiting for them. She asked the guards to remove Kirk's handcuffs and leg irons during the tests. They agreed.

The tests lasted a couple of hours. When Kirk finished, Dr. Salk began to write up the results.

"Can I go out in the hall and have a smoke?" Kirk asked.

The doctor nodded. Kirk stepped out into the hall. Evans and the guards were waiting there. Evans reached into her purse and pulled out two guns. Calmly, she handed a gun to Kirk.

"All right, put your hands on your heads," Kirk told the guards.

The three guards obeyed, and Kirk led them back into Dr. Salk's office. Evans ran to her car to get the tape and clothes. Then she returned to Dr. Salk's office.

In the office, Evans pointed her gun at Dr. Salk. He stared at her in amazement, but she just stared back. She didn't seem to care what he or anyone else thought.

Kirk kept his gun pointed at the four men. Evans cut long strips of tape and handed them to Kirk. He used the tape to tie up the four men. Then Evans cut the cord to the telephone. She waited while Kirk took off his prison uniform and put on the clothes that she had brought.

"Okay, let's go," Kirk said at last.

Lawyer Turns Outlaw (p. 2)

Evans did not hesitate. She knew she was giving up her family, her friends, and her work, but she didn't seem to care. She walked quickly out the door with Kirk. The two of them climbed into her car and drove away.

It took police five months to find Kirk and Evans. They had been living in Florida. In August, they were brought back to Tennessee to stand trial. Tim Kirk was given 40 extra years behind bars. Mary Evans was given three years for helping him escape. As the guards led her to prison, she showed no regret.

Even though the case was closed, it left many questions unanswered. How did Kirk talk Evans into helping him escape? Why was Evans willing to give up so much? No one understood why she had taken the law into her own hands.

FLORIDA

Do You Remember?

In the blank, write the letter of the best ending for each sentence.

_____ **1.** Mary Evans was a

    a. lawyer.   b. nurse.   c. teacher.

_____ **2.** Tim Kirk was in prison for

    a. writing bad checks. b. armed robbery.   c. kidnapping.

_____ **3.** Tim Kirk was taken to Dr. Salk's office by

    a. guards.   b. his sister.   c. a judge.

_____ **4.** Dr. Gary Salk gave Tim Kirk some

    a. guns.   b. sleeping pills.   c. tests.

_____ **5.** Mary Evans and Tim Kirk were found in

    a. Tennessee.   b. Florida.   c. Arkansas.

Lawyer Turns Outlaw (p. 3)

Critical Thinking — Main Ideas

Underline the two most important ideas from the story.

1. Tim Kirk was 36 years old.

2. Tim Kirk convinced his lawyer to help him escape from prison.

3. Mary Evans surprised everyone by running off with Tim Kirk.

4. Tim Kirk asked Mary Evans to bring tape to Dr. Salk's office.

5. Dr. Gary Salk sometimes gave tests to prisoners.

Exploring Words

Choose the correct word from the box to complete each sentence.

armed robbery	regret	trial	hesitate	murdered

1. To _____ means to stop for a moment because of doubt.

2. If someone has been killed on purpose, that person has been _____.

3. To feel badly about something you have done is to feel _____.

4. Using a gun to steal something is known as _____.

5. A court holds a _____ to decide if

someone is guilty or not.

Washed Away!

The rain poured down all night, and rivers flowed over their banks. Main Street was already underwater. By noon on May 31, 1889, some of the people of Johnstown, Pennsylvania, had seen enough. They left for higher ground. Most, however, stayed put—they had been through flood scares before.

Fourteen miles up the valley from Johnstown stood the South Fork Dam. It was built with dirt in the 1840s, and it held back a huge lake. A break in the dam would flood the whole valley. This worried some people. After all, how long could a dam made of dirt last?

Daniel Morrell was one of the most important people in Johnstown. Morrell sent an engineer to look at the dam. The engineer reported a big leak and said the dam needed to be repaired.

Morrell wrote letters to the dam's owners, begging them to fix the dam, but the owners lived far away, in Pittsburgh. They were not worried about the dam. One owner wrote to Morrell, "You and your people are in no danger from our enterprise." Morrell wrote back that the dam was dangerous to the lives and property of all those living in the valley.

Morrell died in 1885. Four years later, his worst nightmare came true.

The heavy rains had filled the lake. At 3:10 P.M. on May 31, the dam gave way.

Twenty million tons of water exploded down the valley, wiping out everything in its path. Along the way, the flood picked up hundreds of trees, houses, and boulders. The flood crashed through the small town of Woodvale in five minutes, killing 314 people. Only one building was left standing.

Johnstown was next in the flood's path. It took about ten minutes for the raging waters to destroy the town. People did what they could to save themselves. Some ran for higher ground, others clung to floating rooftops, and still others ran for the strongest-looking building they could find.

Six-year-old Gertrude Quinn was on the third floor of her house when the flood struck. The house trembled as the water pounded against the walls.

Gertrude managed to climb up on the roof. She jumped onto a mattress that was floating by just as her house was swept away.

Luckily, debris beneath the mattress kept it floating. Night was approaching, and Gertrude was terrified. A dead horse slammed into her raft.

The six-year-old floated by a large building with people crowded on the roof. She screamed for help. A mill worker named Maxwell McAchren heard her. He dived into the water. His head bobbed up and down in the strong current. Several times he went under, but at last he climbed onto the mattress.

Together, the two floated along. Suddenly, they saw two men on a hillside about ten feet away. The men were trying to help people. One of the men shouted, "Throw that baby over here to us."

McAchren picked up Gertrude. Using all his strength, he threw the little girl to

Washed Away! (p. 2)

the shore. One of the men caught Gertrude. McAchren had saved the little girl's life. Later, he also managed to save himself.

By the morning of June 1, the flood was over. It left behind a sea of debris and death. About 2,200 people had died. Thousands of people had no homes, there was little food or medicine, and there was no gas or electricity.

Soon help began pouring in from around the country. People sent food, clothing, candles, blankets, and lumber.

The Army and the Red Cross came to help. Slowly, the people of Johnstown brought their town back to life. But they never rebuilt the South Fork Dam.

Critical Thinking — Fact or Opinion?

A fact can be proven. An opinion is a belief. Opinions cannot be proven. Write _F_ before each statement that is a fact. Write _O_ before each statement that is an opinion.

_____ **1.** People who lived in Johnstown were foolish.

_____ **2.** Daniel Morrell wrote letters to the owners of the dam.

_____ **3.** The South Fork Dam was built in the 1840s.

_____ **4.** Daniel Morrell should have fixed the dam himself.

_____ **5.** The flood hit Woodvale first.

_____ **6.** Gertrude was the luckiest girl in the world.

_____ **7.** Maxwell McAchren liked to swim.

_____ **8.** Many people crowded onto rooftops.

Name _____ Date _____

Washed Away! (p. 3)

Do You Remember?

In the blank, write the letter of the best ending for each sentence.

_____ **1.** The South Fork Dam was built with
   a. bricks.   b. steel.   c. dirt.

_____ **2.** The dam owners lived in
   a. Pittsburgh.   b. Johnstown.   c. Woodvale.

_____ **3.** Gertrude Quinn jumped onto a
   a. horse.   b. mattress.   c. railroad car.

_____ **4.** Maxwell McAchren threw Gertrude to two men
   a. on a roof.   b. in a tree.   c. on the shore.

_____ **5.** The flood killed about
   a. 200 people.   b. 2,200 people.   c. 20,000 people.

Exploring Words

Use the clues to complete the puzzle. Choose from the words in the box.

| dam |
| enterprise |
| nightmare |
| ton |
| raging |
| clung |
| debris |
| terrified |
| current |
| death |

Across
4. movement of water
5. rushing wildly
6. end of life
9. bad dream
10. scattered trash

Down
1. held on
2. very frightened
3. business
7. 2,000 pounds
8. wall to hold back water

Stories of Disaster

A City in Ruins

James Hopper was having a nightmare. He heard the sound of horses running. Then a loud roar shook Hopper out of his bed. A real nightmare had just begun.

The surprised reporter rushed to his hotel window. The building was moving from side to side. Hopper heard the roar of bricks coming down. The rear of the three-story building was falling. It crushed the wooden houses below. This is death, Hopper thought. He waited to see what would happen next.

It was early in the morning of April 18, 1906. The birds were singing. A thin moon hung in the  sky. The morning weather report said, "Fair and warmer." It was 5:12 A.M.

Then, without warning, the earth began to shake violently. Streets rolled like waves in the ocean. Buildings swung violently from side to side and then crashed to the ground.

The earthquake lasted 40 seconds. Ten seconds of silence followed. Then a second earthquake, equal to the first, shook the city. Trains were tossed on their sides. People died instantly as they were crushed under rubble. Some of those who lived found that their fourth-floor windows were now level with the ground.

The streets quickly filled with people.

Most were still in their pajamas. One man ran along the street with his coat and hat, but he had forgotten his pants. A woman wandered through the streets carrying a birdcage with four kittens in it. A black bull, freed by the earthquake, ran down the street.

Some people stood in shocked silence. Others wanted to talk. Maybe if they talked, they could make some sense out of what had happened.

This was the worst earthquake ever to hit the United States. The earthquake caused other problems. It broke gas lines and brought down telephone wires. Worst of all, it broke the main water pipes.

In just a few minutes, dozens of fires started. Because of broken pipes, there was no water to fight the fires. Flames shot up from one end of the city to the other.

Fire horses and engines clattered toward the fires. Firefighters ran from one hydrant to another. Sometimes they would find a hydrant that worked; at other times they would use a well. But many times there was no water to be found.

The flames jumped from housetop to housetop. Smoke climbed high above the city and could be seen 100 miles away.

People grabbed blankets or clothes from their homes. They sat outside their homes waiting. When the fires came too close, they left. Sadly, they dragged whatever they could behind them.

The refugees sat on hilltops watching

A City in Ruins (p. 2)

the fires come toward them. The fires formed a wall three miles long. When the refugees could feel the heat on their faces, they moved on again. There were 250,000 people now without homes.

The fires took everything in their paths. Chinatown went. Flames burned The Emporium, the largest store in the West. Fire shot up the eighteen-story Call Building. It exploded like a firecracker. San Francisco was burning to death.

The mayor of San Francisco was Eugene Schmitz. Many people saw him as a weak leader, but he came out of this crisis a hero. In a strong voice, he gave his orders.

"Is looting a problem? Protect people's property. Order the police and the Army to kill all persons found looting.

"Are people drinking and causing trouble? Then forbid the sale of alcohol."

Schmitz ordered, "Get dynamiters from the Army to blow up buildings in the path of the flames. When the fires reach the ashes, they'll burn themselves out."

The dynamite didn't help much. The fires burned on for three days and turned 510 city blocks into ashes. There was $500 million in property damage and nearly 700 people dead. Four fifths of San Francisco was destroyed.

Finally, it was over. Slowly people began to walk back into the city. They began picking up the rubble. The bricks were still hot and burned their hands. But they could not wait. They took off their coats and rolled up their sleeves.

"Let's go," they said. "Let's get started."

San Francisco would live again.

Do You Remember?

Read each sentence below. Write _T_ if the sentence is true. Write _F_ if the sentence is false.

_____ **1.** The earthquake lasted for hours.

_____ **2.** Many fires broke out after the earthquake.

_____ **3.** There were 250,000 people who lost their homes.

_____ **4.** Chinatown was not damaged.

_____ **5.** Mayor Schmitz ordered the Army to use dynamite.

_____ **6.** Most of San Francisco was destroyed.

Stories of Disaster

Name _____   Date _____

A City in Ruins (p. 3)

Express Yourself

Pretend that you are James Hopper. On a separate piece of paper, write an article for a magazine. Describe what it felt like to live through the earthquake.

Exploring Words

Use the words in the box to complete the paragraphs. Reread the paragraphs to be sure they make sense.

crisis	rubble	shocked	hydrant	violently
forbid	dynamite	refugees	earthquake	looting

The **(1)** _____ hit early in the morning. The ground shook

(2) _____. People were **(3)** _____ to see buildings

fall. Then the city faced a new **(4)** _____. Fire raced through the

city. Firefighters hooked up hoses to any **(5)** _____ that would work.

People became **(6)** _____ as they left their

homes, running from the fires. Some people began

(7) _____ stores.

Mayor Schmitz took action. **(8)** "_____ the sale of alcohol," he

ordered. He also asked the Army to bring in **(9)** _____. At last the

fires stopped. People picked through the **(10)** _____. They began

to build the great city again.

Stories of Disaster

Nonfiction 5, SV 6180-X

Nightmare at Sea

Captain Edward Smith had been given the honor of taking the *Titanic* on her very first trip. After this trip, he planned to retire. Smith told the lookout, Frederick Fleet, about the reports of ice he had received. Then he went inside the ship to dinner.

Fleet searched the darkness. His job was to watch for icebergs. Fleet watched carefully, but he wasn't really worried. The *Titanic* was the biggest, strongest, safest ship ever built. All at once, Fleet saw a black shadow right in front of the ship. It was an iceberg! Quickly he rang the warning bell.

For the next 37 seconds, the crew tried to steer the ship out of the  way, but it was no use. At 11:40 P.M. on April 14, 1912, the iceberg rammed the side of the *Titanic*. Slowly, the huge unsinkable ship started to sink.

Word of the accident spread quickly through the ship. The passengers were confused but not upset. They thought this was a new adventure. A few crew members knew better.

Captain Smith went to check the 16 watertight compartments at the bottom of the ship. The *Titanic* should float even if three or four of them filled with water. Captain Smith found that five of the rooms were now hopelessly flooded. Water was filling the other rooms as well. The *Titanic* was going down.

On the deck, crew members hurried to get out the lifeboats, but they had never had a practice drill. It had not seemed necessary. Finally, they got the first boat ready. Captain Smith called out the order. "Women and children first!"

But most women and children refused to go. They didn't trust the small boats. Many still did not believe the ship was in danger. An hour later, only 20 people were in the first lifeboat. There was room for 45 more people, but the crew could wait no longer. At 12:45 A.M., they lowered the half-empty lifeboat into the water.

Finally, people understood that the *Titanic* was sinking. Suddenly, everyone wanted to get into a lifeboat. But there were not enough to go around. There were 2,207 people on the *Titanic*, but there were only enough lifeboats for 1,178 people.

The shortage of lifeboats brought out the worst in some people. One man snuck into a lifeboat dressed as a woman. Others pushed ahead of mothers and small children. Some men had to be dragged kicking and screaming out of the boats.

But while some people became cowards, others became heroes.

Dr. W.T. Minahan helped his wife into a boat, then stepped back to make room for someone else. "Be brave," he called to his wife. "No matter what happens, be brave."

Someone else tried to help an older man named Isidor Straus into a lifeboat. But Straus shook his head. Mrs. Straus, like many other women, refused to leave

Nightmare at Sea (p. 2)

her husband. "We have been living together for many years," she said. "Where you go, I go." Then the two of them sat down in deck chairs to wait for the end together.

On the deck, the ship's band played. They felt it was their duty to stay with the ship. They tried to comfort the passengers by playing loud, cheerful music.

By 2:00 A.M., all of the lifeboats were in the water. There wasn't much hope left for those still on the ship. Some jumped into the water and tried to swim out to the lifeboats. A few made it, but most quickly died in the freezing water.

One swimmer looked back and saw Captain Smith standing on the ship with water up to his waist.

The bow of the ship was underwater, and the stern was up in the air. At 2:18 A.M., with the band still playing, the great ship sank to the bottom of the ocean, taking more than 1,500 people with it.

The *Titanic's* radio operator had called for help on the ship's radio. The *Carpathia* was the first ship to arrive. Its crew began picking up the people in the lifeboats at 4:10 A.M. Of the 2,207 people who had sailed on the *Titanic*, only 711 were still alive.

The *Titanic* became a legend. For 73 years, people searched for its remains. Finally, on September 1, 1985, a team of French and American explorers found her. The rusty wreck lay two miles under the Atlantic Ocean. She was no longer the beautiful and graceful ship she had once been.

Do You Remember?

Read each sentence below. Write *T* if the sentence is true. Write *F* if the sentence is false.

_____ **1.** The *Titanic* hit an iceberg.

_____ **2.** Captain Smith ordered his crew to get into lifeboats.

_____ **3.** There were not enough lifeboats for everyone.

_____ **4.** Every lifeboat was packed full of passengers.

_____ **5.** The band played songs as the *Titanic* sank.

Nightmare at Sea (p. 3)

Critical Thinking — Main Ideas

Underline the two most important ideas from the story.

1. The *Titanic* sank after it hit an iceberg.

2. Captain Smith was planning to retire.

3. The mail room was filled with water.

4. The *Carpathia* was the first ship to arrive.

5. Many people died because there were not enough lifeboats.

Exploring Words

Write the correct word in each sentence.

unsinkable	watertight	compartments	
lifeboats	shortage	bow	stern

1. When there isn't enough of something, there is a _____.

2. If something is _____, water cannot get in or out of it.

3. The front part of a ship is called the _____.

4. _____ are small boats which people use if they have to leave

the main ship.

5. If something cannot sink, it is

called _____.

6. _____ are small, separate rooms.

7. The back part of a ship is called

the _____.

Hurricane Warning!

Señor Garcia stood at the window. He saw waves tossing and thrashing. "We must go," he whispered to his wife. "The hurricane is coming!"

"No, I will never leave my home," she said.

So the two of them stayed in the little village of La Carbonera, Mexico. The weather grew wilder. The wind reached 120 miles per hour. Señor Garcia had never seen a storm so full of fury.

Suddenly, the hurricane tore into the Garcias' house, ripping off the roof and knocking down walls. Somehow, Señor Garcia escaped injury, but his wife lost her life in the storm.

Hurricane Gilbert was the worst storm to come out of the Atlantic Ocean in 80 years. It began off the coast of Africa in September 1988. At first, it was only a small cluster of thunderclouds, but it gathered strength as it moved over open water. It picked up heat and moisture. When it reached the Caribbean Islands, it was a monster.

By then the storm stretched over 450 miles. It carried heavy rain and strong winds. At the eye of the storm, the wind reached hurricane level—it measured an amazing 175 miles per hour.

This wind was deadly. It smashed buildings, ripped up telephone poles and streetlights, and sent 25-foot waves crashing onto beaches. It even carried a big ship for five miles and dumped it onto the sand.

The island of Jamaica caught the worst of the storm. There the wind tore the roofs off 80 percent of all the homes and left half a million people homeless. It also destroyed crops, banana trees, coconut trees, and sugar cane plants.

As Gilbert approached Jamaica on September 12, tourists rushed to get off the island. Many made it; but hundreds did not. Those who were stuck on the island gathered in big hotels. But even there they were not safe. The storm shattered hotel windows. It broke down walls. It sent furniture flying.

"It was like being hit by an atom bomb," one tourist later said.

"Sixty-foot trees were just plucked out of the earth," another said.

One man summed it up. "There was no power, no water, no phones, nothing. The place was wrecked."

After leaving Jamaica, Gilbert raced through the Cayman Islands. Then it rushed on to Mexico. There the howling wind and rain did new damage. The storm leveled thousands more homes. It flipped cars and ruined roads, and it flooded mile after mile of land.

On September 17, Gilbert finally lost its great strength. The wind died down, and the rain grew lighter. But evidence of the storm remained. It had caused billions of dollars in damages. Over 800,000 people had no homes. The death count reached 300.

Hurricane Warning! (p. 2)

However, things could have been worse. In the past, a hurricane like Gilbert would have killed thousands of people. It would have hit without warning. There would have been no way to predict its path.

This time, at least, everyone knew Gilbert was coming. Weather experts used new tools to study Gilbert's path. These experts sent out plenty of warnings. The warnings gave many people time to flee. Others could at least try to protect themselves and their property from the wind. Luckily, most people lived through Hurricane Gilbert. They were able to dry out and start again after the fury of Gilbert had passed.

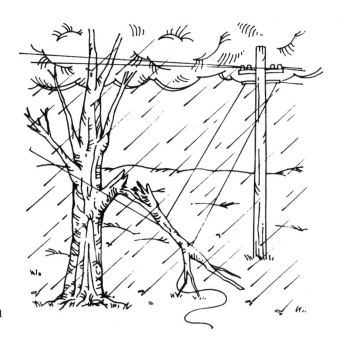

Do You Remember?

In the blank, write the letter of the best ending for each sentence.

_____ **1.** Hurricane Gilbert began off the coast of

      a. Canada.   b. China.   c. Africa.

_____ **2.** The hurricane did the most damage in

      a. England.   b. Jamaica.   c. New Mexico.

_____ **3.** Hurricane Gilbert destroyed Jamaica's crop of

      a. bananas.   b. potatoes.   c. rice.

_____ **4.** The hurricane caused

      a. snowdrifts.   b. flooding.   c. fires.

_____ **5.** Weather experts were able to give people

      a. raincoats.   b. free food.   c. warning.

Hurricane Warning! (p. 3)

Express Yourself

Pretend that you were a tourist in Jamaica. You were trapped on the island by Hurricane Gilbert. On a separate piece of paper, write a letter to a friend telling what happened and how you felt.

Exploring Words 🔍

Find the best meaning for the word in dark print. Fill in the circle next to it.

1. The word **thrashing** means
   ⓐ moving wildly.   ⓑ cooking.   ⓒ singing.

2. The word **hurricane** means
   ⓐ hard candy.   ⓑ high speed.   ⓒ a bad windstorm.

3. The word **fury** means
   ⓐ wild and dangerous force.   ⓑ ready to eat.   ⓒ striped.

4. The word **cluster** means
   ⓐ dirty.   ⓑ a group of something.   ⓒ a ring.

5. The word **percent** means
   ⓐ out of each hundred.   ⓑ buy.   ⓒ gift.

6. The word **evidence** means
   ⓐ proof.   ⓑ whirlwinds.   ⓒ trash.

7. The word **predict** means
   ⓐ wonder.   ⓑ tell what will happen.   ⓒ win a bet.

8. The word **flee** means
   ⓐ fly.   ⓑ run away.   ⓒ doesn't cost money.

Doctor for the Poor

In 1954, Tom Dooley, a young Navy doctor from America, stood in a camp in Vietnam for refugees from the French Indochina War. The camp was crowded with sick, hungry people. They had diseases that had been wiped out long ago in most parts of the world. Almost all were tired and dirty and poor. Dooley stayed in the camp for several months. He gave the refugees medicine and bandaged their cuts. Most important, he showed them kindness.

Dooley later wrote, "I saw more sickness in a month than most doctors see in a lifetime."

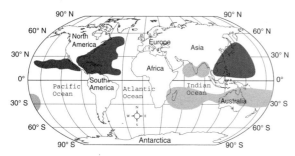

By the time he left the Navy in 1955, Dooley knew he could not be happy living in the United States again. The U.S. didn't really need another doctor. But in Southeast Asia, doctors were desperately needed. Dooley went to Laos, the country just west of Vietnam, to set up a small hospital.

Dooley knew Laos was a poor country. Still, life there came as a shock to him. Laos was even poorer than Vietnam. There was just one real doctor in the whole country. Many of the two million Laotians used witch doctors. Many more got no help at all.

In 1956, Dooley opened his hospital in the village of Vang Vieng. Three other Americans helped him. Norman Baker, Peter Kessey, and Dennis Shepard had worked with Dooley at the refugee camp in Vietnam.

Word of Dooley's hospital spread quickly. Every morning Laotians lined up for sick call. They had no money, so they carried chickens, eggs, and vegetables to give to Dooley. These people had every kind of sickness. Dooley could cure some of them. All Dooley could do for others was to make them feel more comfortable.

In the afternoons, Dooley went out on jeep call. He took his jeep to nearby villages and honked his horn. The sick would crawl out of their huts to get help from him.

Dooley saw many people die because they didn't get medicine in time. Sometimes he would wonder if he was doing any good. Then he would glance up at the picture of a 14-year-old girl named Savong. The picture of Savong kept Dooley in Laos.

Dooley first met Savong in 1956. An American man was driving along a jungle trail when some Laotians stopped his jeep. They took him to Savong, who was lying on the ground, almost dead. He put the girl in his jeep and rushed her to Dooley.

Savong's leg had been badly scratched. No one had cleaned the wound. Soon an infection developed, and as it spread, Savong grew sicker and sicker. Dooley had seen many poor, dying children in Asia. Many of them were beyond help,

Doctor for the Poor (p. 2)

but he thought Savong had a chance. After many hours in surgery, he had done all he could; the rest was up to Savong.

Dooley, Baker, Kessey, and Shepard took turns watching over the girl. One day she smiled, then she began to cry. She couldn't believe she was still alive. After she became strong and well, Savong returned to her village. Her picture stayed on Dooley's wall.

In January 1957, Dooley left Vang Vieng. He turned the hospital over to Laotians he had trained. Dooley wanted to open a new hospital in Nam Tha, a village high in the mountains. Nam Tha was poorer than Vang Vieng. It had no roads. Supplies had to be brought in by plane or carried in on foot. Dooley's hospital was nothing more than a simple bamboo hut.

Dooley treated dozens of people every day. Some came to the hospital; many others were too sick to travel. So Dooley often packed up his bag and traveled to the villages. Many times, he had to walk an hour or more to reach them. He had to climb steep rocks and cross rope bridges. At the end of each day, he was exhausted. But he was happy to see how much he was helping the people of Nam Tha.

One of the hardest parts of his job was dealing with the people Dooley called witch doctors. These witch doctors often made a sick person even sicker. They rubbed pig grease into cuts and covered burns with dirt.

Dooley knew they should not do this, but he did not want to anger the witch doctors. He knew the Laotians trusted them. He tried to show them how important it was to wash their hands and keep cuts clean. In time, he helped them learn a few rules of modern medicine.

After three years in Southeast Asia, Dooley's own health began to fail. He went to New York for help. The doctors found he had cancer. "I'm not going to quit," he said. "I will continue to guide and lead my hospitals until my back, my brain, my blood, and my bones collapse."

Dooley went back to Laos, but by December 1960, he was very sick. He returned to a New York hospital. There, on January 18, 1961, he died. His life had been short, but he had done much to help the people of Southeast Asia.

Express Yourself ✎

Pretend you are a reporter who has been sent to interview Tom Dooley at his hospital in Nam Tha. What questions would you ask Dr. Dooley? Write your questions of a separate piece of paper.

Doctor for the Poor (p. 3)

Do You Remember?

Read each sentence below. Write *T* if the sentence is true. Write *F* if the sentence is false.

_____ **1.** Dooley went to Laos because he couldn't find work in the United States.

_____ **2.** Dooley saved Savong's life.

_____ **3.** Laotians often paid Dooley with eggs and vegetables instead of money.

_____ **4.** Dooley did not allow Laotians to work in his hospitals.

_____ **5.** Dooley died of cancer.

Exploring Words

Use the words in the box to complete the paragraphs. Reread the paragraphs to be sure they make sense.

infection	surgery	refugees
collapse	cancer	witch doctors

Tom Dooley worked in Vietnam in a camp for **(1)** _____. Later he moved to Laos and opened his own hospital. He saved many lives. He saved the life of a girl with a bad **(2)** _____ in her leg by performing **(3)** _____ on her.

Dooley also worked with Laotian **(4)** _____ and was able to teach them some rules of modern medicine.

After three years in Laos, Dooley learned he had **(5)** _____. He said he would keep helping Laotians until his **(6)** _____.

Beating the Odds

Five-year-old Evonne Goolagong sat on the steps of her parents' house in Barellan, Australia, watching some older children batting a tennis ball around. "When will I be able to play tennis?" she asked her mother.

"Evonne," said her mother sadly, "you know we don't have money for things like tennis rackets."

Evonne knew her mother was right. The Goolagongs were very poor. Evonne's father worked shearing sheep and didn't make much money. Sometimes he couldn't even afford to feed his eight children. Evonne knew he could never afford to buy her a tennis racket. Still, she kept dreaming of tennis. To her, it seemed like the most wonderful game in the world.

One day Evonne picked up an old broomstick and a tennis ball. "Look, Mum!" she cried happily. "This broomstick can be my tennis racket!"

For the next few months, Evonne practiced with the broomstick. Then an aunt found out how much Evonne loved tennis and gave her a racket as a present. Evonne was thrilled. "I used to sleep with that racket," she later said. She played with it every chance she got.

Evonne played at the Barellan War Memorial Tennis Club. It had a dusty dirt court with a sagging net. Hour after hour Evonne played there. Bill Kurtzmann, the club president, noticed how good she was. He started to help her with her tennis. In 1961, he entered 10-year-old Evonne in a small tournament. It turned out that the tournament was for women, not girls, but Evonne didn't care. She decided to play against the women. She won easily.

Clearly Evonne had a special talent, but what could she do with it? She was a poor Aborigine. Aborigines are black Australians. Their history is much like that of the Native Americans. The Aborigines settled in Australia long before white people, but whites later drove them off the land. Most ended up in barren parts of Australia. As a result, most Aborigines are poor, with little hope for the future.

Like many other Aborigines, Evonne seemed trapped by her family's poverty. Talent scouts came to watch her. They could see she had real talent, but without good training, she could not become a top player. And the Goolagongs couldn't afford good training.

In 1961, Vic Edwards heard about Evonne. Edwards was the best tennis teacher in Australia. He invited Evonne to spend a few weeks at his club in Sydney. The Goolagongs couldn't afford to send her. "I'm sorry, Evonne," said her father. "We just don't have the money."

The Goolagongs' friends and neighbors wanted to help Evonne. They could see she was special. They believed in her and her talent. Quickly they raised money to buy Evonne new clothes and a plane ticket. They sent her off to Edwards' club in Sydney.

Stories of Heroes

Beating the Odds (p. 2)

With Edwards' help, Evonne became better and better. When she was 14 years old, Edwards went to see her parents. He asked if Evonne could come live with his family year-round. "That way she could have the training she needs," he said.

The Goolagongs agreed. They wanted to give Evonne the chance to follow her dream. From then on, Edwards worked with Evonne every day. He helped her with her tennis game and made sure she studied hard and finished high school.

By the time she was 19 years old, Evonne was a big name in the world of tennis. Between 1968 and 1970, she won 44 tournaments in Australia. In 1971, she won the French Open. Her friends and family back in Barellan cheered each time they heard of a Goolagong victory. "Soon she'll be the best in the world," they said to each other.

Vic Edwards was thinking the same thing. In August of 1971, he entered Evonne in England's Wimbledon tournament. This was the most important tournament in the world. "Good luck," he said to her as Wimbledon began. "And remember—you're not really alone out there. There are a lot of people who believe in you."

Evonne easily won the early rounds. In the final match, she faced Margaret Court. Court was a white Australian and the best woman tennis player in the world. Could Evonne beat her?

On the day of the big match, Evonne played brilliantly. She beat Court by winning two straight sets. This was only the beginning. Goolagong continued to win tournaments throughout the 1970s. She showed that money and race are not important. She proved that with talent, hard work, and good friends, anything is possible.

Do You Remember?

Read each sentence below. Write _T_ if the sentence is true. Write _F_ if the sentence is false.

_____ **1.** For several months, Evonne used a broomstick as a tennis racket.

_____ **2.** Vic Edwards didn't think Evonne had talent.

_____ **3.** Evonne's neighbors raised money so Evonne could get good training.

_____ **4.** Evonne's parents refused to let her play tennis.

_____ **5.** Evonne never beat Margaret Court.

_____ **6.** In 1971, Evonne won the Wimbledon tennis tournament.

Stories of Heroes

Beating the Odds (p. 3)

Express Yourself

Pretend you are one of Evonne Goolagong's parents. Would you let Evonne live with Vic Edwards' family? Why or why not? Write your thoughts on a separate piece of paper.

Exploring Words

Read each sentence. Fill in the circle next to the best meaning for the word in dark print. You may use a dictionary.

1. Evonne's father worked **shearing** sheep.
   - ⓐ moving
   - ⓑ cutting wool off
   - ⓒ killing

2. Evonne played at the Barellan War **Memorial** Tennis club.
   - ⓐ in honor of
   - ⓑ for members only
   - ⓒ indoor

3. The club had a dusty dirt court with a **sagging** net.
   - ⓐ huge
   - ⓑ new
   - ⓒ falling down

4. Vic entered Evonne in a small **tournament**.
   - ⓐ contest
   - ⓑ book
   - ⓒ journey

5. Clearly Evonne had a special **talent**.
   - ⓐ language
   - ⓑ skill
   - ⓒ job

6. The Aborigines' history is much like that of **Native** Americans.
   - ⓐ enemies of
   - ⓑ born in a place
   - ⓒ angry

7. They ended up in the most **barren** parts of Australia.
   - ⓐ where things don't grow
   - ⓑ filled with people
   - ⓒ beautiful

8. Most Aborigines had little hope for the **future**.
   - ⓐ yesterday
   - ⓑ the time yet to come
   - ⓒ today

9. Evonne seemed trapped by her family's **poverty**.
   - ⓐ orders
   - ⓑ money
   - ⓒ having no money

10. She beat Court by winning two straight **sets**.
    - ⓐ groups of games
    - ⓑ bets
    - ⓒ chairs

Answer Key Nonfiction Grade 5

Assessments
P. 7
1. a
2. b
3. a
4. c
5. b
P. 8
Answers will vary.
P. 9
A. 1, 4
B. 1. opinion
2. fact
3. opinion
4. fact
5. fact
P. 10
A. Answers may vary.
Examples:
1. they wanted more freedom.
2. it did not hold the air.
3. it was too risky.
B. 1. false
2. true
3. true
4. false
5. true
Pp. 12-13
Do You Remember?
1. c
2. b
3. c
4. a
Critical Thinking
1. O
2. F
3. O
4. O
5. F
Exploring Words
1. b
2. c
3. c
4. a
5. c
6. b
7. a
8. b
Pp. 15-16
Critical Thinking
Answers will vary.
Examples:
1. African officials wouldn't let Jane live in the wilderness alone.
2. she hoped to learn the secrets of how chimpanzees behaved.
3. leopards and buffalo in the forest might attack if they were startled.
4. she wanted to learn all she could about them.
Do You Remember?
1. a
2. b
3. c
4. a
5. c
Exploring Words
1. officials
2. discouraged
3. progress
4. malaria
5. fever
6. sweat
7. figs
8. groom
9. male
10. emotions

Pp. 18-19
Do You Remember?
1. b
2. c
3. a
4. c
Express Yourself
Answers will vary.
Exploring Words
Across:
3. miles per hour
7. death
8. entire
9. deadly
10. oxygen
Down:
1. hurled
2. braking
4. sideways
5. altitudes
6. system
Pp. 21-22
Do You Remember?
1. b
2. c
3. a
4. b
5. c
Express Yourself
Answers will vary.
Exploring Words
1. equipment
2. assistance
3. cigarette
4. explosion
5. hull
6. dreadful
7. explosives
8. flinch
9. experience
10. ram
Pp. 24-25
Do You Remember?
1. F
2. T
3. T
4. F
5. T
Critical Thinking
3, 4
Exploring Words
Across:
2. tissue
4. scars
6. heroism
7. treatment
9. cerebral palsy
10. percent
Down:
1. operation
3. especially
5. ambulance
8. clung
Pp. 27-28
Do You Remember?
1. T
2. T
3. T
4. F
5. T
Critical Thinking
Answers may vary.
Examples:
1. the fuel system started to leak and oil spurted onto a hot pipe.
2. the fire was out of control and would soon burn the entire ship.

3. it heard the *Prinsendam's* SOS.
4. some of them were older and had health problems.
Exploring Words
1. a
2. b
3. b
4. c
5. b
Pp. 30-31
Do You Remember?
1. b
2. c
3. c
4. a
5. b
Critical Thinking
1, 5, 2, 4, 3
Exploring Words
1. microphone
2. solid
3. jackhammer
4. progress
5. drill bits
6. grave
7. alert
8. nightmare
Pp. 33-34
Critical Thinking
Answers may vary.
Examples:
1. she felt the Union needed her.
2. she heard there were not enough doctors in the field.
3. they were busy with wounded soldiers.
4. the people were suffering.
Do You Remember?
1. T
2. T
3. F
4. F
5. T
Exploring Words
1. b
2. a
3. c
4. b
5. b
6. a
7. c
8. b
Pp. 36-37
Express Yourself
Answers will vary.
Do You Remember?
1. c
2. b
3. a
4. c
5. a
Exploring Words
1. hardships
2. horizons
3. ambition
4. competition
5. compass
6. altitude
7. shock wave
Pp. 39-40
Do You Remember?
1. T
2. T
3. F
4. F
5. T

Critical Thinking
1, 3, 5, 4, 2
Exploring Words
1. seriously
2. surgery
3. rhythm
4. edgy
5. current
6. natural
7. pace
8. enormous
Pp. 42-43
Do You Remember?
1. b
2. a
3. b
4. c
5. a
Express Yourself
Answers will vary.
Exploring Words
1. interview
2. dozed
3. photographer
4. checkpoints
5. recover
6. nylon
7. grueling
8. raged
9. struggled
10. Conditions
Pp. 45-46
Critical Thinking
1. O
2. F
3. O
4. F
5. F
Do You Remember?
1. c
2. b
3. b
4. a
5. c
Exploring Words
1. bandit
2. advanced
3. engineers
4. serpents
5. inspired
6. advisers
Pp. 48-49
Do You Remember?
1. T
2. F
3. T
4. F
5. T
6. F
7. T
8. F
Critical Thinking
2, 4
Exploring Words
Across:
1. glorious
5. carrier pigeon
7. illness
9. varnish
10. fate
Down:
2. odor
3. excellent
4. gracefully
6. equipment
8. seams

Answer Key Nonfiction Grade 5 (p. 2)

Pp. 51-52
Do You Remember?
1. b
2. a
3. b
4. c
5. a
Express Yourself
Answers will vary.
Exploring Words
Across:
2. ancient
6. warnings
7. desperately
8. sap
Down:
1. backwards
3. coral reef
4. balsa
5. currents
Pp. 54-55
Do You Remember?
1. c
2. b
3. a
4. b
5. b
Critical Thinking
1. F
2. O
3. F
4. O
5. F
Exploring Words
1. a
2. c
3. a
4. c
5. b
6. a
Pp. 57-58
Do You Remember?
1. F
2. T
3. T
4. T
5. T
6. F
7. F
8. F
Express Yourself
Answers will vary.
Exploring Words
Across:
3. countless
5. material
8. details
9. tombs
10. soil
Down:
1. scraping
2. enormous
4. triangles
6. lizard
7. positions
Pp. 60-61
Do You Remember?
1. F
2. F
3. T
4. F
5. T
6. F
7. T
8. T

Critical Thinking
1 and 3
Exploring Words
1. quarry
2. stunned
3. survive
4. sculptors
5. moai
6. culture
Pp. 63-64
Do You Remember?
1. F
2. T
3. T
4. F
5. T
Critical Thinking
Answers may vary.
Examples:
1. everything was in place but the crew of the ship was missing.
2. there were no storms in the area and no wreckage was ever found.
3. they couldn't see anything and their instruments stopped working.
4. the instruments had stopped working while they were in the Triangle.
Exploring Words
1. b
2. c
3. a
4. a
5. b
6. b
Pp. 66-67
Do You Remember?
1. F
2. T
3. T
4. F
5. F
Express Yourself
Answers will vary.
Exploring Words
Across:
5. natives
8. rumors
9. navigator
Down:
1. landmarks
2. base
3. frantically
4. mission
6. grave
7. anchored
Pp. 69-70
Do You Remember?
1. b
2. a
3. a
4. b
5. c
Critical Thinking
2, 4, 1, 3, 5
Exploring Words
1. a
2. c
3. c
4. b
5. c
6. b

Pp. 72-73
Do You Remember?
1. b
2. b
3. a
4. c
Express Yourself
Answers will vary.
Exploring Words
1. Communists
2. inflate
3. taffeta
4. vowed
5. height
6. clues
Pp. 75-76
Do You Remember?
1. a
2. b
3. a
4. c
5. b
Critical Thinking
2, 3
Exploring Words
1. hesitate
2. murdered
3. regret
4. armed robbery
5. trial
Pp. 78-79
Critical Thinking
1. O
2. F
3. F
4. O
5. F
6. O
7. O
8. F
Do You Remember?
1. c
2. a
3. b
4. c
5. b
Exploring Words
Across:
4. current
5. raging
6. death
9. nightmare
10. debris
Down:
1. clung
2. terrified
3. enterprise
7. ton
8. dam
Pp. 81-82
Do You Remember?
1. F
2. T
3. T
4. F
5. T
6. T
Express Yourself
Answers will vary.
Exploring Words
1. earthquake
2. violently
3. shocked
4. crisis
5. hydrant
6. refugees
7. looting

8. Forbid
9. dynamite
10. rubble
Pp. 84-85
Do You Remember?
1. T
2. F
3. T
4. F
5. T
Critical Thinking
1, 5
Exploring Words
1. shortage
2. watertight
3. bow
4. Lifeboats
5. unsinkable
6. Compartments
7. stern
Pp. 87-88
Do You Remember?
1. c
2. b
3. a
4. b
5. c
Express Yourself
Answers will vary.
Exploring Words
1. a
2. c
3. a
4. b
5. a
6. a
7. b
8. b
Pp. 90-91
Express Yourself
Answers will vary.
Do You Remember?
1. F
2. T
3. T
4. F
5. T
Exploring Words
1. refugees
2. infection
3. surgery
4. witch doctors
5. cancer
6. collapse
Pp. 93-94
Do You Remember?
1. T
2. F
3. T
4. F
5. F
6. T
Express Yourself
Answers will vary.
Exploring Words
1. b
2. a
3. c
4. a
5. b
6. b
7. a
8. b
9. c
10. a

Answer Key

Nonfiction 5, SV 6180-X